THE BOOK OF
Chinese
COOKING

THE BOOK OF
Chinese
COOKING

JASPER SPENCER-SMITH

Photography by
RAYMOND BRAGG

PUBLISHED BY
SALAMANDER BOOKS LIMITED
LONDON

Published by Salamander Books Limited
8 Blenheim Court, Brewery Road, London N7 9NY

© Salamander Books Ltd., 1991, 2001

A member of the Chrysalis Group plc

ISBN 1 84065 121 0

This book was created by Pegasus Editions Limited,
Premier House, Hinton Road, Bournemouth, Dorset BH1 2EF

Editor: Hilary Walden
Designer: Paul Baker
Home Economist: Moo Leng Loakes
Photographer: Raymond Bragg
Typeset by: Shirley Westerhoff
Colour separations by: Aero Offset (Bournemouth) Limited
Printed and bound in Spain

ACKNOWLEDGEMENTS:

The publisher would like to thank the following for their help and
advice:

Neal Street East, Neal Street, Covent Garden, London
Braun
Sabatier
Le Creuset

Note:
All spoon measurements are equal.
1 teaspoon = 5 ml spoon.
1 tablespoon = 15 ml spoon.

CONTENTS

INTRODUCTION

The testimony to the inherent quality and appeal of Chinese cooking is the way it has captured the imagination and respect of cooks, top chefs and food-lovers throughout the West. This is hardly surprising since it is one of the richest, many-faceted and purest cuisines in the world.

The unique style of sophisticated simplicity has been developed over centuries through the expertise of one of the world's oldest, most advanced civilisations.

The vast, varied landmass and long coastline of China provide a wealth of diverse, natural foods, which Chinese cooks, with their deep reverence for the 'fruits' of nature, have cleverly and carefully transformed into a variety of styles. These span the whole spectrum, from the subtle delicacy of steamed dim sum to the fiery piquancy of Szechuan Hot and Sour Soup.

Chinese cooks have drawn on their culinary knowledge to create the most suitable, delicious, yet economical uses for every food, and they have discovered the best ways of combining foods to emphasise to perfection textures, tastes, colours and aromas. Rich foods are counterbalanced by bland ones, brightly coloured ingredients are juxtaposed with pale, smooth textures contrasted by crunch, and a hot dish by a cold one.

Despite its 5,000 year old roots, Chinese cooking is right up-to-date. It is fresh, light, practical and relevant to today's lifestyles and needs.

The Chinese do not believe in over-elaboration, preferring to allow the food to speak for itself. Cooking equipment is simple, kept to a minimum, and makes efficient use of heat.

Through authentic recipes, THE BOOK OF CHINESE COOKING captures the essential, living spirit of true Chinese food, and enables you to take advantage, today, of centuries of experience to recreate with ease, in your own kitchen masterly, harmonious dishes.

REGIONAL CHINESE COOKING

China is a vast country extending from the sub-tropical regions of Hunan and Kwantung in the south right up to the dry plains of Mongolia in the north, whilst the western borders go right into central Asia, reaching almost to the frontier of Afghanistan. Being so large there are dramatic contrasts in geography and climate across the country. The great diversity of regional history, customs, life and culture have caused a distinct cuisine to evolve in each of the four major provinces.

NORTH

The cooking of Peking and northern China is a fusion of three distinct influences, high-class court and mandarin dishes, rustic Mongolian and Manchurian fare, and the indigenous cooking of the cold, northerly climate. Consequently, variations in the refinement, elegance and lightness of the foods can be noticed.

Throughout the area, though, rice has taken a back seat to wheat. This is immediately apparent in the number and variety of pancakes, noodles, dumplings, breads and buns that are to be found everywhere. Stir-frying is less common, but barbecueing, lacquer roasting, spit-roasting, slow-simmering and deep-frying are popular.

Sauces are richly flavoured with dark soy sauce, garlic, green onions and spices; and sesame oil is used more frequently than elsewhere.

Lamb, a meat largely disliked elsewhere in China, is eaten in northern areas due to the Mongolian influence.

WEST

The Szechuan cuisine tends to be hearty rather than delicate, and is renowned for highly spiced foods, especially dishes containing chillies. Szechuan cooks have also perfected a fascinating range of hot-sour, savoury-spiced and sweet-hot-piquant recipes. Many are characterized by the crunch and bite of pickles, for in this inland region the preservation of foods by pickling in salt and vinegar is popular, as is smoking.

Unlike many dishes in eastern China, in the west a number of dishes are fried with only enough sauce to convey seasonings, and so the sauce itself is not an important element of the dish. As a result, dishes are drier and more reminiscent of southern stir-fries.

Multiple flavours are another feature in the cuisine of the west, and it is quite usual to find garlic, chillies, vinegar and soy sauce in one dish.

EAST

The cooking of the east is more starchy, and richer — not only in the amount of lard and oil used in cooking (although this is usually either left in the pan, or allowed to fall to the bottom of the bowl and not eaten), but also in the range of ingredients, the amount of soy sauce, and number and combinations of spices.

Another significant characteristic is the heavier use of rice. Not only is it served plain as an accompaniment, but is also combined with vegetables, and used as a stuffing. Rice-based products such as the widely used rice wine, exist in profusion. With a long coastline, and well-watered lands, a fine selection of seafood and plenty of freshwater fish are caught. A great range of vegetables is also available.

People of Shanghai are sweet-toothed and use sugar fairly liberally, making savoury dishes that are generally sweeter than elsewhere.

SOUTH

To many people, the cooking of Canton is exemplified by stir-frying in a wok. But this is only part of the picture. Southern cooking is probably the most inventive, rich and colourful in China. It has been influenced by a steady stream of foreign traders and travellers, and is richly endowed with year-round produce from land and sea, thanks to the sub-tropical climate and longest coastline of the Chinese provinces.

Fruits flourish and are combined in meat and savoury dishes more here than elsewhere. Vegetables are used in quantity, but meat sparsely. As well as stir-frying, steaming and roasting are prevalent and the use of oil in cooking kept to a minimum. Every meal includes rice, and exotic ingredients such as shark's fin and birds nests are common. Southern dishes are often sauced with thick but delicate sauces.

The area produces some of the best soy sauce in the country, and, because of this, specialises in 'red cooking', slowly baking or braising in soy sauce until the liquid has evaporated, to add an attractive red colour to the food.

CHINESE MEALS

When composing a meal, as when composing a dish, Chinese always consider the contrasts between the flavours, colours, textures and aromas of all the dishes, and make sure they achieve a good balance. Chinese also distinguish between salty, sweet, sour, hot, bitter, bland, aromatic and cool. The dipping sauces and seasonings on a table can add a dramatic touch to the occasional mouthful.

The number of dishes served at a Chinese meal will depend on the number of diners; generally there is one course per diner. Dishes are not served in any particular order, but tend to arrive as they are cooked. Soups are not served at the start of a meal; instead, they come somewhere in the middle or even at the end as their function is to wash down the rice. In some meals there may be two soups, the first being served as a second course. As a general rule, an everyday Chinese meal will not finish with a sweet, although there may sometimes be fruit. However at the end of banquets or elaborate feasts there may be a dessert.

Dishes are communal, with everyone helping themselves to portions of everything.

As each dish must be within the reach of everyone, round tables are used, often with rotating centres, so no-one has to stretch to reach any dish.

Dim sum, which literally means 'little heart' or 'to dot the heart', are eaten only at lunchtime or as snacks at odd times of the day, even just before going to bed. Traditionally, they would not be eaten at a main meal, although their popularity in the West has caused many restaurants to flout tradition. Dim sum can be sweet or savoury, they can be deep-fried, poached, baked or braised, but most often they are steamed dumplings with various fillings which come to the table in round wooden or bamboo containers piled one on top of each other. Dim sum may also be miniature versions of a main course dish, such as tiny spare ribs or baby pancake rolls.

INGREDIENTS

All of the ingredients used in THE BOOK OF CHINESE COOKING can be bought readily from Chinese food shops and special delicatessens. An increasing number, some of which may even be from a Western source, can also be found in good supermarkets. Those that are not are usually added as optional ingredients or alternatives suggested.

VEGETABLES

Bean sprouts – these small, young tender shoots are usually mung beans that have germinated, although other beans can also be allowed to sprout. Bean sprouts are nutritious, containing generous amounts of vitamins and minerals, and add a delicious crunch to stir-fry dishes.
Chinese beans – the tender pods of these green beans can be eaten whole. Snap beans or French beans can be substituted.
Chinese cabbage (bok choy) — the most widely available of Chinese green vegetables. The stalks have a mild, refreshing flavour, and the leaves are pleasantly tangy with a slight bitterness.
Chinese flowering cabbage (choy sum) — very similar to 'bok choy', though slightly smaller, with narrower stalks and slightly paler green leaves; the distinctive feature is the yellow flowers. These are cooked with the rest of the vegetables.
Celery cabbage (wong ah bok) — delicate pale green vegetable with a sweet taste that makes it ideal for use in salads. Its delicate flavour blends superbly with other foods.
Coriander – fresh coriander resembles flat-leaved parsley in appearance, but it smells and tastes very different. Both of these are quite distinctive, and not immediately appealing to some people, but it does not take long for any initial reservations to be overcome and can quickly become a firm favourite.

Fresh coriander wilts quickly so buy as near as possible to the time of using; or grow your own.
Daikon – daikon is the Far Eastern variety of winter radish that is also called 'mooli'. Being long, white and fat it looks more like a giant carrot than the small, round, red radish that is commonly seen in the West. Daikon is eaten both raw in salads, and cooked in vegetable dishes. It is also pickled.

FRUIT

Lychees – canned lychees are a 'staple' dessert in many Chinese restaurants. But when making Chinese meals at home, look for fresh lychees as they are now becoming far more readily available. They need no more preparation than using the fingers to easily crack the nobbly, brittle coating. Beneath it, delicious, crisply-fruity glistening white flesh surrounds a smooth central stone. Neither the skin nor the stone are eaten.
Mango – there are many different types of mango, each one varying in size, shape and colour. But whichever is available, select fruit that feels heavy for its size and is free of bruises or damage. A ripe mango yields to gentle pressure and should have an enticing, scented aroma. The flesh inside should have a wonderful, luxurious and slightly exotic texture and flavour, but poor quality fruit can be disappointing; the key is the fragrance.

If a mango is a little firm when bought, leave it in a warm sunny place to finish ripening.
Star fruit – star-fruit are long, almost translucent yellow, ridged fruit; they are also known as 'carambola'. The whole fruit is edible, and when cut across the width, the slices resemble five-pointed stars. Raw star-fruit have a pleasant, citrus-like, juicy sharpness, but when poached the flavour is more distinctive.

CORNFLOUR MIXTURE

Measure spoons of cornflour into a bowl, then stir in twice the amount of water. Pour into a screw-top jar and keep in the refrigerator. Stir or shake jar before measuring out required amount.

INGREDIENTS

Black beans, salted fermented — these very salty soy beans are available in cans and plastic packages.

Chinese five-spice powder — a warmly aromatic blend of spices.

ChingKiang vinegar — the most well-known brand of Chinese black vinegar. Black vinegars are made from grains other than rice, and aged to impart complex, smoky flavours with a light, pleasant bitterness. Substitute sherry, balsamic vinegar or a good red wine vinegar.

Gingko nuts — these have a hard shell, which must be removed before cooking, and a creamy-coloured flesh. Shelled gingko nuts are also available in cans. If unavailable, substitute almonds.

Hoisin sauce — a reddish-brown sauce based on soy beans, and flavoured with garlic, chillies and a combination of spices. Flavours vary between brands, but it is nearly always quite sweet and it can range from the thickness of a soft jam to a runny sauce.

Mushrooms — Chinese cooks seldom buy fresh mushrooms, preferring to use dried ones. These must be soaked before cooking — put the mushrooms into a bowl, cover with boiling water, cover the bowl, leave for about 20-30 minutes until swollen and pliable, then drain well. If the stems are tough, discard them.

Winter black mushrooms — with a fairly intense, fragrant flavour, these are the most widely used.

Cloud ear — also known as 'wood ear', these are added for their texture rather than flavour, as they have little.

Straw — these thin, tall, leaf-like mushrooms are also known as 'paddy straw' or 'grass' mushrooms. They are canned as well as dried.

Oyster sauce — made from oysters, salt, seasonings and nowadays, cornflour and colouring.

Pickled and preserved vegetables — various types of vegetables, preserved, or pickled, in salt, are available in cans and plastic pouches, but if a label simply specifies '*Preserved Vegetable*', it will invariably mean mustard greens.

Turnip — these are not Western turnips, but a type of radish.

Rice vinegar — the mildest of all vinegars, with a sweet, delicate flavour and comes in several varieties. If possible, use a pale rice vinegar for light coloured sweet-and-sour dishes, and try a dark variety for dipping sauces. If unable to find either, use cider vinegar.

Rice wine — similar to sherry in colour, bouquet and alcohol content (18%), but with its own distinctive flavour. Shaoshin is the most famous brand. Substitute a good dry sherry if unavailable.

Rose Wine — imparts an exotic quality to foods. Use sweet sherry as a substitute.

Soy sauce — made from fermented soy beans, a good soy sauce has a rich aroma and a salty, pungent flavour that heightens other flavours.

Many qualities and grades are available. Many mass-produced ones are chemically fermented hydrolized protein, but they can easily be detected. A thick, foamy head that takes quite a while to disperse will form on the top when the bottle is shaken vigorously, whereas the bubbles on top of a chemically-fermented product fade quickly.

Dark soy is used with dark meats and dipping sauces; light soy with vegetables, seafood and soups.

Sesame oil — this is made from toasted sesame seeds. The thicker and browner the oil, the more aromatic it is. Sesame oil enlivens other flavours. Care is needed when cooking with sesame oil as it tends to burn easily; Chinese cooks usually sprinkle a few drops over a dish immediately before removing from the heat.

Shrimp paste — concentrated, salty and with a pronounced shrimp-like flavour and smell.

Star anise — a dark brown, dried 8-pointed star-shaped spice. It has a distinctive aniseed flavour, with liquorice overtones.

Szechuan peppercorns — reddish coloured, with a mildly hot flavour, and a spicy fragrance reminiscent of coriander seeds. Buy whole seeds if possible as the flavour deteriorates more quickly once they have been ground.

Yellow bean paste — made from fermented soy beans, it is salty and pungent and may be chunky or smooth.

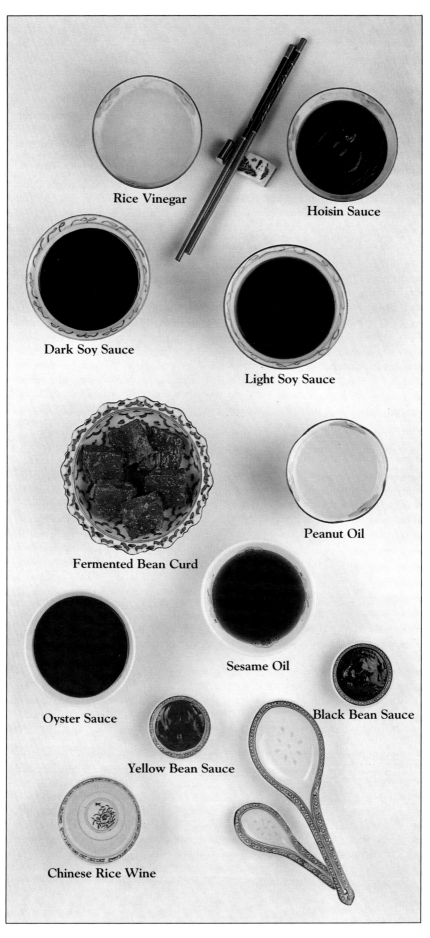

Rice Vinegar

Hoisin Sauce

Dark Soy Sauce

Light Soy Sauce

Fermented Bean Curd

Peanut Oil

Oyster Sauce

Sesame Oil

Black Bean Sauce

Yellow Bean Sauce

Chinese Rice Wine

─── CHINESE EQUIPMENT ───

Chinese cooks often spend more time in the kitchen preparing the ingredients than in cooking them. Cooking utensils are few, practical and versatile, and are designed to make the most efficient and economical use of heat.

Chopping board – a planed slice of tree, about 37.5 cm/15 in in diameter and 20-25 cm/8-10 in height, is the preferred choice of Chinese chefs for a chopping board, but an ordinary, heavy board will be perfectly satisfactory for normal domestic kitchens in the West.

Cleaver – Chinese cooks use a cleaver for all tasks that require a knife, from carving delicate flower shapes from vegetables to chopping bones. A Chinese chef selects the cleaver that has the right size and weight for his physique. Frequent honing on a stone ensures that it is always razor-sharp.

Chopsticks, for cooking – special long chopsticks are used for cooking, particularly stir-frying.

Chopsticks, for eating – the important points to remember are that there is an upper and a lower chopstick, the lower one should always be held stationary, and the square ends should be held pointing upwards and the rounded or tapered ends downwards.

Pick up the chopsticks as you would a pen or pencil and let an equal amount of the chopstick protrude on each side of the hand. Now, instead of holding the chopsticks with your thumb and index finger, as you would hold a pencil, hold with the tips of the fourth and the little finger and let the upper part of the chopstick rest comfortably in the base of the thumb and the index finger. This is the stationary chopstick.

With your other hand, pick up the second chopstick and place directly above the first, and parallel to it. Hold the upper stick firmly with the thumb, index and middle fingers as you would a pencil. Use the thumb to brace the stationary chopstick securely against the tip of the fourth finger. There should be about 2.5 cm/1 in of space between the sticks. Press the upper chopstick down with the index and third finger

so that it meets the stationary chopstick to pick up the food. Tap the ends of the chopsticks gently on the table to make sure they are even as chopsticks will not work efficiently unless aligned.

Skimmer – shallow, wide, metal mesh skimmers are used for lifting deep-fried food from the oil, and for serving pieces of food from 'pot-style' meals.

Spatula – for efficiency, safety and comfort when stir-frying a spatula with a curved blade that follows the contours of the wok, and a long handle that allows the hand to be kept away from the heat, is used.

Steamers – Chinese cooks use bamboo steamers, that have no bottom, and are designed to sit over a wok. Often two or more steaming baskets are stacked on top of each other so that a number of dishes can be cooked at the same time. The steam is absorbed by the bamboo lid preventing water dripping onto the food. So that all the nourishing juices and flavour are retained, the food is often placed on a plate in the steamer and served directly from it.

Whisk – a whisk about 25 cm/10 in long and consisting of thin strips of bamboo tied together at the top, rather like a witches broomstick, is used for cleaning a wok.

Wok – the wok is the cornerstone of Chinese cooking. Woks come in many sizes. They are curved like a shallow bowl, are made of iron, copper or stainless steel, and have two handles on opposite sides. The flared sides permit easy, rapid tossing of a number of ingredients and the use of the minimum of oil, not only for stir-frying but also deep-frying.

To hold the wok steady it is placed on a metal, perforated ring. If you have a gas stove, place the ring right-side up on the stove, but if you cook by electricity, turn the ring so the bottom is uppermost. Electric woks are also available. As well as stir-frying, woks are used for deep-frying, braising, steaming, boiling, crystal-boiling and red cooking. A wok is often supplied with a domed lid for using when braising, red cooking and crystal-boiling.

Wire ladles – these are used for cooking Potato Baskets, page 105.

——WESTERN EQUIPMENT——

Whilst it may make a cook feel that they are being truly authentic if they use Chinese utensils, it is not necessary to buy any special equipment. The equipment that is available in the average Western domestic kitchen is quite adequate for the preparation and cooking of a whole range of Chinese dishes.

Frying pans – ordinary frying pans can be used in place of a wok. A light-weight frying pan is preferable for stir-frying as it will heat up quickly and convey the intense heat that is required. The most practical pans are those that are wide and have deep sides, as they allow the food to be tossed and stirred more easily. They will also prevent the various ingredients from being too close together, which slows down the cooking and can hamper the food becoming crisp.

Chopping board – a conventional, heavy wooden chopping board can be used quite satisfactorily.

Food processor – a food processor with a selection of slicing discs is very useful for quickly, neatly and evenly slicing and chopping for stir-frying.

Kitchen knives – a selection of sharp, strong-bladed knives will help with the quick, efficient cutting and slicing of ingredients.

Slotted spoon – can be as effective as a wire skimmer for removing food from deep oil or cooking liquids.

Steamer – a Western-style steamer can be used in place of a bamboo steamer, but it is a good idea to line the lid with kitchen paper to prevent drips of water falling onto the food.

Tongs – tongs can be used for turning and lifting food, instead of cooking chopsticks.

—— COOKING TECHNIQUES ——

Stir-frying – the essentials for good stir-frying are very little oil, food that is finely sliced or shredded with every piece cut to the same size, the use of a fierce heat so the food is cooked quickly, and tossing the ingredients.

The wok is put over a high heat, a little oil is poured and when really hot, the flavouring vegetables, such as garlic and ginger, are added. After a few seconds stirring, the meat goes into the wok, is stirred and tossed for a minute then removed. Next come the vegetables in the order of the length of cooking they require. When they have all been stirred and tossed for the requisite time, the meat is returned to the wok, and seasonings added. The food must then be served immediately to preserve its crispness.

Deep frying – Chinese deep-frying is done in a wok, so uses less oil. Foods are often marinated first in soy sauce and spices, and then sometimes coated in batter; a mixture of cornflour and egg white is the most usual. Often, the food is fried until almost cooked, then removed from the oil, the oil reheated and the food added again to finish cooking and become really crisp.

Steaming – steaming is far more popular in China than in the West and is used to cook meat, poultry, fish, dim sum, other pastries and desserts. It was developed as a fuel saving measure as several foods can be cooked at once in baskets, which in China are made of bamboo, stacked above each other. Foods that require the most cooking are put to cook first, and those needing less time are placed on top in succession, as the cooking proceeds.

Red cooking – food, usually in large pieces, is cooked slowly in dark soy sauce, sometimes with other flavourings added. During the lengthy cooking, which may be as long as 4 hours, the soy imparts a fairly dark, reddish brown colour and a rich flavour to the food. Because of the large amount of soy sauce that is used, the food can also be salty, so sugar may be added to counteract it.

Roasting – few domestic kitchens in China have an oven so roast Chinese dishes are usually those that are made in restaurants or the homes of well-to-do families.

—— VEGETABLE CUTTING ——

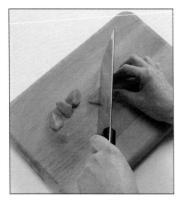

ROLL CUTTING

Cut a diagonal slice from the vegetable. Make a one-quarter turn of the vegetable towards you and make a diagonal slice slightly above and partly across the face of the first slice. Continue until vegetable is completely cut.

DIAGONAL CUTTING

Using a Chinese cleaver, or sharp heavy-bladed chef knife, hold the knife at 45 degree angle to the surface of the food, and slice across diagonally, at a 45 degree angle. Move the knife along the length of the width of slice desired; make another cut, and continue along the length of the food.

SHREDDING

Cut the sides and ends of the vegetables so that they are flat. Hold the vegetables firmly with the fingertips. Work the knife across the vegetables, moving the blade up and down and just in front of the fingers, moving the fingers along the vegetable closely followed by the knife. Cut the vegetable lengthwise across the slices to the width of a matchstick.

PREPARING PRAWNS

In China, deepwater prawns are used. These are larger than the prawns most commonly seen in the West, which are freshwater prawns. Mediterranean or jumbo prawns are the best type to use when making Chinese recipes. The dark vein that runs down the back of the prawn must always be removed before the prawn is eaten.

Break off or cut off the head if present, then slip off the body shell and remove the legs; the tail section may be left on. (The heads and shells can be reserved for cooking).

Run the point of a sharp knife lightly down its back and carefully pull away the dark vein; discard.

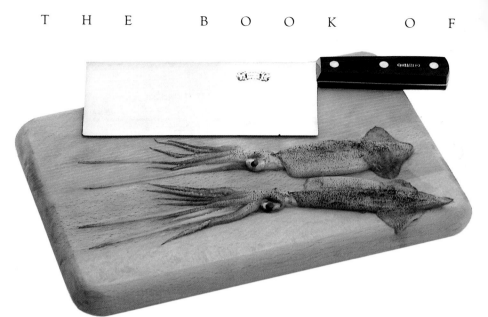

PREPARING SQUID

Squid are very popular in China and are sold fresh and frozen (squid freeze well) in all Chinese fish markets.

Plump, large squid are preferred for their flavour, texture and the decorative appearance they can add to a dish. The tentacles are cut across their width so the slices resemble stars; they are then used in stir-fry dishes, tossed in salads or coated in batter and deep-fried.

Thoroughly rinse the squid. Holding the head just below the eyes, gently pull it away from the body pouch, bringing the ink sac and other soft viscera with it. Discard the body pouch, but reserve the ink sac if desired.

Ease back the edge of the body pouch to locate the fine, stiff 'pen', then pull it out and discard.

Cut the tentacles from the head just below the eyes; discard the head. Cut away the cartilage at the base of the tentacles. Squeeze off the beak-like mouth in the centre of the mass of tentacles.

Peel off the skin of the body pouch, then cut away the edible fins. Rinse the squid, then cut across the body into slices.

SPRING ROLL SKINS

125 g (4 oz/³/₄ cup) plain (all-purpose) flour
55 g (2 oz/¹/₂ cup) cornflour (cornstarch)
3 tablespoons vegetable oil
440 ml (14 fl oz/1 ³/₄ cups) water
600 ml (1 pint/2 ¹/₂ cups) vegetable oil for frying

In a bowl, mix together the flour and cornflour (cornstarch) then gradually stir in the water and oil to make a smooth batter.

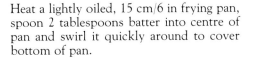

Heat a lightly oiled, 15 cm/6 in frying pan, spoon 2 tablespoons batter into centre of pan and swirl it quickly around to cover bottom of pan.

Cook until the pancake is dry but not coloured and the edges shrink from the sides of the pan.

Transfer to a plate, cover with a damp cloth. Repeat until all the batter has been used.

To fill the skins, lay one out flat on a work surface. Place a portion of filling slightly off-centre.

Fold the sides of the skin neatly over the filling, then roll up to enclose the filling completely. Brush around the edges with beaten egg to seal.

Makes 20 spring roll skins.

CHINESE OMELETTE

2 eggs

In a bowl, lightly beat together the eggs. Heat a dry, preferably non-stick, small frying pan.

Pour in the eggs, stir lightly while tipping the pan so the raw egg flows onto the dry area.

Cook for about 2 minutes until the underside is set and the top still slightly liquid. Turn the omelette over and cook the other side for about 2 minutes, until set.

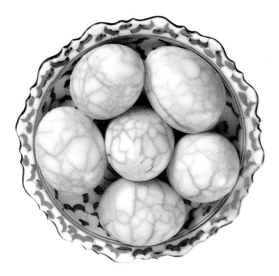

TEA EGGS

8 eggs
3 tablespoons Keemun black tea
1 tablespoon sea salt
1 teaspoon Chinese five-spice powder
2 tablespoons dark soy sauce

Boil eggs, just covered by water for 8-10 minutes. Cool under cold running water for 5 minutes. Roll and tap the eggs gently to crack their shells, but do not detach the shells from the eggs.

In a saucepan just large enough to hold the eggs in a single layer, mix tea, salt, five spice powder and soy sauce with enough water to cover the eggs; bring to the boil.

Place eggs in pan and simmer for 30 minutes. Turn off the heat and leave eggs to cool completely in the mixture. Peel off the shells to serve.

Serves 4.

PORK DIM SUM

450 g (12 oz) minced pork
115 g (4 oz) raw shelled prawns, ground
1 ¹/₂ tablespoons soy sauce
¹/₂ tablespoon Chinese rice wine or dry sherry
¹/₂ tablespoon sesame oil
¹/₂ tablespoon sugar
Dash of pepper
1 egg white
1 ¹/₂ tablespoons cornflour (cornstarch)
30 wonton skins
Fresh or frozen green peas or chopped
      hard-cooked egg yolks, for garnish

To make filling: Mix together ground
pork, ground prawns, soy sauce, rice wine
or sherry, sesame oil, sugar, pepper and
egg white until mixture is well blended
and smooth. Stir in cornflour. Divide
into 30 portions. Cut off the edges of
wonton skins to form circles, if necessary.
Place 1 portion of filling in the middle of a
wonton skin. Gather the edges of the
wonton skin around the meat filling. Dip
a teaspoon in water and use to smooth the
surface of the meat.

Garnish by placing a green pea or
chopped egg yolk on top of meat. Gather
the edges to form a waist. Repeat with
remaining wonton skins and meat filling.
Line a steamer with a damp cloth; steam
over high heat 5 minutes. Remove and
serve.

Makes 30 dumplings.

PRAWN DIM SUM

450 g (12 oz) raw shelled prawns, ground
115 g (3 oz) can bamboo shoots, chopped
4 tablespoons water
1 $^1/_2$ tablespoons soy sauce
$^1/_2$ tablespoon Chinese rice wine or dry sherry
$^1/_2$ teaspoon sugar
$^1/_2$ teaspoon sesame oil
Dash of pepper
1 $^1/_2$ tablespoons cornflour (cornstarch)

Dough:
450 g (12 oz/2 $^1/_2$ cups) plain (all-purpose) flour
115 m (4 fl oz/$^1/_2$ cup) boiling water
70 ml (2 $^1/_2$ fl oz/$^1/_3$ cup) cold water
1 tablespoon vegetable oil

To make filling: Mix together all ingredients except cornflour until the mixture is well blended and smooth.   Stir in
cornflour.   Divide into 30 portions.

To make dough: Put 315 g (10 oz/2
cups) of the flour in a medium size bowl.
Reserve remaining flour and use for hands
if they become sticky.   Stir in the boiling
water.   Add the cold water and oil.   Mix
to form dough; knead until smooth.   Roll
the dough into a long, rope shape and cut
it into 30 pieces.   Use a rolling pin to roll
each portion into a thin 5 cm (2 in) circle.

Place 1 portion of the filling in the middle
of a dough circle.   Bring the opposite
edges together and pinch them together to
hold.   Repeat with remaining circles and
filling.

Line a steamer with a damp cloth.   Set the
Har Gau about 2.5 cm (1 in) apart.   Steam
over high heat 5 minutes.   Remove and
serve.

Makes 30 dumplings.

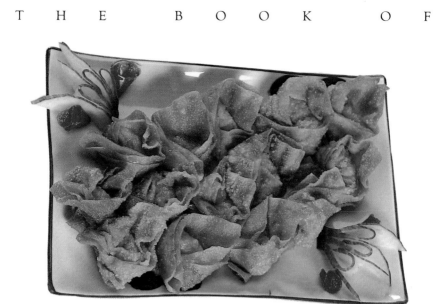

FRIED WONTONS

185 g (6 oz) minced pork
115 g (3 oz) can water chestnuts, finely chopped
1 tablespoon water
1 tablespoon cornflour (cornstarch)
$^1/_2$ teaspoon salt
$^1/_2$ teaspoon Chinese rice wine or dry sherry
Dash of sesame oil
Dash of pepper
30 wonton skins
Vegetable oil for frying

To make filling: Mix together all ingredients except wonton skins and vegetable oil until meat and water chestnuts are combined into a uniform mixture. Divide into 30 portions.

Put 1 tablespoon of the filling in the middle of a wonton skin. Diagonally fold the skin in half to form a triangle. Fold the edge containing the filling over about 1 cm ($^1/_2$ in). Bring the 2 points together, moisten one inner edge and pinch the edges together to hold. Repeat with remaining wontons and filling.

Heat a wok, then add the vegetable oil. Deep fry the wontons over a medium heat until golden. Drain on paper towels and serve.

Makes 30 wontons.

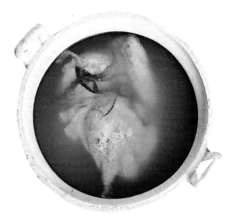

— CHINESE CHICKEN STOCK —

¹/₂ chicken
1 bacon hock, split
4 slices root ginger
4 spring onions, chopped
1 tablespoon chopped parsley
2 litres fresh water

Place all ingredients in a large saucepan and bring to the boil. Skim. Reduce heat so liquid simmers, cover gently and cook for 3 hours.

Pour into a sieve lined with muslin, placed over a large bowl. Leave to cool completely. Store, covered, in the refrigerator, or freeze in convenient quantities.

Makes 1.75 litres (58 fl oz/7 cups).

Note: Chinese cooks use Chicken Stock for fish dishes (they do not make fish stock). If fish stock is preferred, substitute a favourite recipe.

– CHINESE VEGETABLE STOCK –

2 tablespoons vegetable oil
1 slice fresh root ginger, peeled
250 g (8 oz) beansprouts
125 g (4 oz) carrots, sliced
15 g ($^1/_2$ oz) dried straw mushrooms, soaked in
    hot water for 20 minutes, drained
60 g (2 oz) dried black winter mushrooms,
soaked in hot water for 25 minutes
1 teaspoon rice wine or dry sherry
2 litres (64 fl oz/8 cups) water
2 teaspoons sea salt

In a large saucepan heat oil, add ginger and fry for 2 minutes. Add the beansprouts and stir-fry for 2 minutes.

Stir in remaining ingredients, bring to the boil, reduce heat so liquid simmers, cover and cook gently for 45 minutes. Pour through a sieve lined with muslin, placed over a large bowl. Leave to cool completely, skim oil from surface and store in the refrigerator for up to 3 days, or freeze in convenient quantities.

Makes 2 litres (64 fl oz/8 cups).

MUSHROOM SOUP

24 dried black winter mushrooms, soaked in hot
    water 25 minutes, drained
1 cm (½ in) piece fresh root ginger, peeled and
    cut into 6 slices
2 spring onions, finely chopped
1.5 litres (48 fl oz/6 cups) Chinese Chicken
    Stock, page 29
2 teaspoons rice wine or dry sherry
1½ teaspoons sea salt
1 teaspoon brown sugar
parsley to garnish

Trim the mushrooms and place in a small
saucepan with half the ginger and half the
spring onions. Add ½ teaspoon salt and
cover with cold water. Bring slowly to the
boil, then simmer for 3 minutes.

Drain. Pour stock into a medium
saucepan, add mushrooms and remaining
ingredients. Bring slowly to the boil,
cover, and simmer gently for 30-35
minutes. Serve hot garnished with
parsley.

Serves 4.

— LAMB & CUCUMBER SOUP —

1 tablespoon dark soy sauce
1 teaspoon sesame oil
250 g (8 oz) lamb fillet, cut into strips
1.5 litres (48 fl oz/6 cups) Chicken Stock,
    see page 29
½ teaspoon sea salt
white pepper
185 g (6 oz) cucumber, cut into paper thin slices
1 tablespoon rice vinegar

In a bowl, mix together soy sauce and sesame oil. Stir in lamb to coat and leave for 30 minutes. Bring chicken stock to the boil; season with salt and pepper. Reduce heat so stock just simmers.

Lift lamb from bowl, add to stock and poach for 2 minutes. Remove lamb and keep warm. Add cucumber to pan and return to the boil. Reduce heat so stock simmers, add lamb and vinegar and cook for 4 minutes.

Serves 4.

CHICKEN & ASPARAGUS SOUP

500 ml (16 fl oz)/2 cups) Chicken Stock, page 29
275 g (12 oz) cooked chicken breast meat,
   finely sliced
90 g (3 oz) canned asparagus tips, drained
   and chopped
2 tablespoons cornflour (cornstarch) mixture, see
   page 10
90 g (3 oz) canned sweetcorn, drained
1 ½ teaspoons sea salt
12 button mushrooms, sliced
1 teaspoon sesame oil to serve
2 spring onions, finely chopped to garnish

In a saucepan bring chicken stock to the
boil.   Add the mushrooms, simmer
for 2-3 minutes then stir in cornflour
(cornstarch) mixture and simmer, still
stirring until thickened.   Reduce heat,
add chicken, asparagus and sweetcorn
and heat through gently but thoroughly.
Season with salt.

Serve sprinkled with sesame oil and garnished with chopped spring onions.

Serves 4.

—— HOT AND SOUR SOUP ——

4 dried black winter mushrooms, soaked in hot
    water for 25 minutes
90 g (3 oz) Szechuan preserved vegetables,
    finely sliced
90 g (3 oz) Chinese pickled green vegetables,
    finely sliced
3 spring onions, finely chopped
3 slices fresh root ginger
850 ml (26 fl oz/3 ¼ cups) water
1 ½ teaspoons rice wine or dry sherry
1 tablespoon light soy sauce
2 cakes tofu, finely sliced
1 tablespoon cornflour (cornstarch) mixture, see
    page 10
1 teaspoon sesame oil

Drain mushrooms, discard stalks, squeeze
out all the liquid, then slice very finely.

In a medium saucepan,   bring all the
ingredients except cornflour (cornstarch)
mixture and sesame oil to the boil;
cook for 3 minutes.   Stir in cornflour
(cornstarch) mixture, simmer, still stirring,
until thickened then add sesame oil.

Serves 4.

- ASPARAGUS AND BEEF SOUP -

1 litre (32 fl oz/4 cups) Chinese Chicken Stock,
   see page 29
2 tablespoons rice wine or dry sherry
1 ½ teaspoons sea salt
2 tablespoons cornflour (cornstarch) mixture, see
   page 10
125 g (4 oz) fillet steak, very thinly sliced
ground white pepper
90 g (3 oz) drained canned asparagus tips,
   coarsely chopped
2 egg whites, lightly beaten

In a large saucepan, bring chicken stock, 1
tablespoon rice wine or dry sherry and ½
teaspoon salt to the boil. Reduce heat
so the liquid barely simmers and stir in
cornflour (cornstarch) mixture. Bring to
the boil, stirring and boil until thickened.
Reduce heat so liquid simmers.

Season steak with 1 teaspoon salt, 1
tablespoon rice wine or dry sherry and
pepper. Add asparagus and steak to the
stock and cook for 10 minutes. Return to
the boil and stir in the egg whites in a thin
stream.

Serves 4.

MEATBALL SOUP

500 g (1 lb) pork tenderloin, finely minced
3 dried black winter mushrooms, soaked in hot
  water for 25 minutes, drained and finely
  chopped
2 spring onions, very finely chopped
2 tablespoons light soy sauce
sea salt
90 g (3 oz/²/₃ cup) cornflour (cornstarch) for
  coating
½ teaspoon ground black pepper
3 tablespoons peanut oil
2 litres (64 fl oz/8 cups) Chinese Chicken Stock,
  see page 29
chopped parsley to garnish

In a bowl, mix together pork, mushrooms, spring onions, soy sauce and 1 teaspoon salt. Pass through the finest blade on a mincer. Roll mixture into 2.5 cm (1 in) balls. Roll balls in cornflour (cornstarch) to lightly coat.

In a wok, heat oil and fry the balls for about 4 minutes until lightly and evenly browned. Drain on absorbent kitchen paper. In a saucepan, heat chicken stock to the boil. Reduce heat so stock simmers, then add meatballs. Season with salt and pepper. Garnish with chopped parsley.

Serves 4.

CRISPY SEAWEED

875g/(1 ³/₄lb) young spring (collard) greens
625 ml (20fl oz/2¹/₂ cups) vegetable oil
1 tablespoon brown sugar
¹/₂ teaspoon sea salt
¹/₂ teaspoon ground cinnamon
90 g (3 oz/ ³/₄ cup) flaked almonds to garnish,
if desired

Remove the thick ribs from the leaves and discard.

Wash the leaves and drain and dry thoroughly with absorbent kitchen paper. Using a very sharp knife or Chinese cleaver cut the leaves into very fine shreds. In a wok heat the oil until smoking, then remove from heat and add greens. Return to a medium heat and stir for 2-3 minutes, or until the shreds begin to float.

Using a slotted spoon remove from the oil and drain on absorbent kitchen paper. In a small bowl, mix together sugar, salt and cinnamon. Place 'seaweed' on a dish and sprinkle with the sugar mixture. Serve cold garnished with flaked almonds, if desired.

Serves 4.

PRAWN TOASTS

30 g (1 oz) pork fat, finely minced
185 g (6 oz) peeled prawns, finely minced
¼ teaspoon sea salt
1 tablespoon cornflour (cornstarch)
1 egg white, lightly beaten
white pepper
3 thin slices white bread, crusts removed
125g (4 oz) sesame seeds
625ml (20 fl oz/2 ½ cups) vegetable oil

In a bowl, mix together fat, prawns, salt, cornflour (cornstarch) and egg white. Season with white pepper.

Spread on to one side of each slice of bread. Coat with a thick layer of sesame seeds, and press well into the spread. Cut each slice into 4 triangles.

In a wok, heat oil until smoking, reduce heat slightly, then carefully lower in the fingers, coated side down. Deep-fry for 2-3 minutes until golden brown. Drain on absorbent kitchen paper. Serve hot.

Serves 4.

CHICKEN LIVERS WITH PRAWN SAUCE

250 g (8 oz) chicken livers, washed
250 g (8 oz) raw prawns with shells
60 ml (2 fl oz/¼ cup) Chinese rose wine or sweet
   sherry
2 tablespoons vegetable oil
1 hot fresh green chilli, seeded if desired, finely
   sliced
2.5 cm (1 in) piece fresh root ginger, peeled and
   grated
1 teaspoon yellow bean paste
1 tablespoon cornflour (cornstarch) mixture, see
   page 10

Bring a small saucepan of water to the boil, add livers and cook for 2 minutes; drain, cool and slice. Shell and de-vein prawns (see page 19). Place shells and heads in a saucepan with 250 ml (8 fl oz/1 cup) water and simmer for 30 minutes. Stir in wine or sweet sherry, strain and reserve liquid.

In a wok, heat oil, add chilli and ginger and fry for 30 seconds, add livers and stir-fry for 3-4 minutes. Using a slotted spoon, remove from wok and drain on absorbent kitchen paper. Add prawns to wok and stir-fry for 2 minutes then return livers, chilli and ginger to wok and cook for 2 minutes. Stir in reserved prawn liquid and bean paste and simmer for 5 minutes. Stir in the cornflour (cornstarch) mixture and bring to the boil, stirring.

Serves 4.

—— SWEET & SOUR TOFU ——

375 g (12 oz) tofu
2 egg whites
2 spring onions, finely chopped
1 teaspoon sesame oil
sea salt and ground white pepper
½ teaspoon brown sugar
250 g (8 oz) canned water chestnuts, chopped
4 dried black winter mushrooms, soaked in hot
  water for 25 minutes, drained
1 teaspoon finely chopped carrot, if desired
125 g (4 oz) cornflour (cornstarch) then add in 2
  tablespoons cornflour (cornstarch) for coating
625 ml (20 fl oz/2 ½ cups) peanut oil
2 spring onions, chopped, to serve

Sauce:
1 tablespoon tomato purée (paste)
2 tablespoons rice vinegar
2 tablespoons fresh orange juice
2 teaspoons light soy sauce
5 teaspoons brown sugar

In a food processor or blender, process
tofu, then work in 1 egg white, the spring
onions, sesame oil, salt, pepper and sugar.
Add water chestnuts, mushrooms, carrot, if desired, remaining egg white and
cornflour (cornstarch) and mix well.

Transfer to a greased 15 cm (6 in)
sandwich tin, levelling surface roughly.
Place in a steaming basket, cover basket,
place over a wok or saucepan of boiling
water and steam for 10 minutes until firm.
Remove from heat and leave to cool.

Cut into bite-sized pieces, toss in cornflour (cornstarch) to coat evenly and lightly.

In a wok, heat oil, add tofu pieces and deep-fry for 5 minutes until golden. Drain on absorbent kitchen paper, place on a warmed serving plate and keep warm.

Pour oil from wok, leaving just 1 tablespoonful. Stir in sauce ingredients and bring to the boil. Pour over tofu cubes and sprinkle with chopped spring onion.

Serves 4.

SPRING ROLLS

20 Spring Roll Skins, see page 22
1 litre (32 fl oz/4 cups) vegetable oil

Filling:
3 tablespoons peanut oil
250 g (8 oz) bean sprouts
6 spring onions, thinly shredded
125 g (4 oz) carrots, cut into thin sticks
125 g (4 oz) button mushrooms, thinly sliced
1 clove garlic, very finely chopped
1 cake tofu, finely chopped
^{1}/4 teaspoon Chinese five-spice powder
1 tablespoon light soy sauce
1 teaspoon sea salt

To make the filling, in a wok heat peanut oil and stir-fry vegetables, garlic and tofu for about 1 minute. Add five-spice powder, soy sauce and salt and continue stir-frying for 2 minutes. Allow to cool.

Make the rolls, see page 22.

In a wok or deep-fat frying pan, heat vegetable oil until smoking. Reduce heat slightly, add 4 spring rolls and fry for 4 minutes, until crisp and golden. Drain on absorbent kitchen paper. Keep warm. Re-heat oil, reduce heat and cook 4 more spring rolls. Repeat with remaining rolls.

Variation: Use 185 g (6 oz) chopped, prepared prawns, see page 19, in place of the tofu.

Serves 4.

— PEKING CHICKEN WINGS —

12 chicken wings
500 ml (16 fl oz/2 cups) peanut oil
125 ml (4 fl oz/½ cup) Chinese Chicken Stock,
    see page 29
2 spring onions, finely chopped
1 tablespoon oyster sauce
1 tablespoon cornflour (cornstarch) mixture, see
    page 10

Marinade:
1 tablespoon dark soy sauce
1 tablespoon peanut oil
1 tablespoon Chinese rose wine or sweet sherry
1 cm (½ in) piece fresh root ginger, peeled and
    grated
2 cloves garlic, peeled and crushed

Place the wings in a saucepan, cover with water, bring to a simmer and cook for 20 minutes. Drain and place in a dish. In a small bowl, mix together marinade ingredients. Pour over chicken wings. Leave for 1 hour, then drain thoroughly; reserve the marinade.

In a wok, heat oil, add wings and deep-fry for 10 minutes until golden brown. Using a slotted spoon, remove wings from oil and drain on absorbent kitchen paper. Pour oil from wok then add chicken wings, stock, spring onions, reserved marinade and oyster sauce. Gently cook for 5 minutes. Stir in cornflour (cornstarch) mixture, bring to the boil, stirring, and simmer until thickened.

Serves 4.

CLAMS WITH SOY & SESAME DIP

1 kg (2 lb) clams in shells, scrubbed and rinsed
1 teaspoon sea salt
4 spring onions, finely chopped
3 cm (1 ½ in) piece fresh root ginger, peeled and
  finely chopped
4 tablespoons dark soy sauce
1 teaspoon medium sherry
2 tablespoons sesame oil

Bring a large saucepan of salted water to a rapid boil, add clams and boil for 10 minutes until clams have opened. Drain, remove and discard the top shells.

Sprinkle each clam with spring onions and ginger. In a bowl mix together the soy sauce, sherry and sesame oil. Spoon a little over each clam.

Serves 4.

— DEEP-FRIED CRAB CLAWS —

4 large crab claws
315 g (10 oz) prepared raw prawns, see page 19,
    minced
½ teaspoon sea salt
pinch of ground white pepper
1 teaspoon cornflour (cornstarch)
1 egg white
125 g (4 oz/1 cup) dried white breadcrumbs to
    coat
625 ml (20 fl oz/2 ½ cups) peanut oil

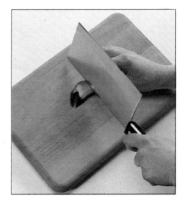

Crack and remove the main shell from each claw, leaving the pincer part intact. Bring a large saucepan of salted water to the boil. Add crab claws, return to the boil and boil for 1 minute. Drain and refresh under cold running water.

In a bowl, mash to an even paste the prawns, salt, pepper, cornflour (cornstarch) and egg white. Divide into 4 portions and press a portion around each claw, leaving pincer showing.

Place breadcrumbs on plate, roll claws in breadcrumbs to evenly coat. In a wok, heat oil, add claws and fry for 10 minutes until golden brown. Drain on absorbent kitchen paper.

Serves 4.

KUNG PO PRAWNS

500 g (1 lb) prepared raw prawns, see page 19
5-6 tablespoons water
4 tablespoons cornflour (cornstarch)
625 ml (20 fl oz/2 ½ cups) peanut oil
2 spring onions, finely chopped
1 cm (½ in) piece fresh root ginger, peeled and
    finely chopped
1 tablespoon rice wine or dry sherry
1 tablespoon light soy sauce
1 teaspoon brown sugar
2 teaspoons sherry vinegar
sea salt and black pepper

In a bowl, stir water into cornflour (cornstarch) to make a light batter. Dip prawns in batter to coat evenly; allow excess batter to drain off.

In a wok, heat oil until smoking, add prawns and deep-fry for about 3 minutes until golden brown. Using a slotted spoon, remove and then drain on absorbent kitchen paper. Pour oil from wok, leaving just 2 tablespoonsful. Add spring onions and ginger and stir-fry for 1 minute. Stir in remaining ingredients and bring to the boil. Add prawns to sauce and heat gently until sauce has thickened.

Serves 4.

PHOENIX PRAWNS

8 large prawns, prepared, see page 19
2.5 cm (1 in) piece fresh root ginger, peeled and
    grated
3 spring onions, chopped
2 tablespoons rice wine or dry sherry
1 teaspoon sesame oil
1 tablespoon light soy sauce
½ teaspoon sea salt
625 ml (20 fl oz/2 ½ cups) vegetable oil

Batter:
4 egg whites
2 tablespoons cornflour (cornstarch)
2 tablespoons plain flour
approximately 185g (6 oz) dry breadcrumbs, for
    coating

Using a cleaver or large knife slightly flatten prawns along their length; place in a dish.In a bowl, mix together ginger, spring onions, rice wine or dry sherry, sesame oil, soy sauce and salt. Pour over prawns and leave for 30 minutes. Make batter in a bowl by beating together the egg whites until thick, then beat in the cornflour (cornstarch) and flour.

Dip prawns in batter to coat thickly and evenly, then coat well with dry breadcrumbs.

In a wok heat vegetable oil until very hot, add prawns and deep-fry for 5 minutes until golden. Drain on absorbent kitchen paper.

Serves 4.

──── PRAWN CHOW MEIN ────

250 g (8 oz) dried egg noodles
2 eggs, beaten
2 tablespoons vegetable oil
1 medium onion, sliced
6 dried black winter mushrooms, soaked in hot
    water for 20 minutes, drained and squeezed
10 canned water chestnuts, sliced
125 ml (4 fl oz/½ cup) Chinese Vegetable Stock,
    see page 30
125 g (4 oz) Chinese cabbage, shredded
500 g (1 lb) shelled cooked prawns
1-2 tablespoons cornflour (cornstarch) mixture,
    see page 10

Boil egg noodles in salted water accord-
ing to pack instructions, drain and keep
warm. Meanwhile, use the eggs to make 2
thin Chinese Omelettes, see page 24.

In a wok heat oil, add onion, water
chestnuts and mushrooms, and stir-fry
for 3 minutes. Stir in stock and cabbage
and cook for 3 minutes. Add prawns;
stir in cornflour (cornstarch) mixture,
bring to the boil, stirring, and simmer
until thickened. Place noodles in a
warmed bowl, pour over the prawns and
vegetables. Thinly slice Omelettes and
scatter over prawns and vegetables.

Serves 4.

—— SZECHUAN PRAWNS ——

500 g (1 lb) prepared raw prawns, see page 19
2 tablespoons vegetable oil
1 clove garlic, finely chopped
1 small fresh red chilli, seeded if desired, finely
   chopped
1 ½ teaspoons chilli sauce
¼ teaspoon cornflour (cornstarch)
¼ teaspoon sea salt
¼ teaspoon brown sugar
2 tablespoons Chinese Chicken Stock, see
   page 29

Bring a large saucepan of salted water to
the boil, add prawns, boil for 1 minute
then drain. In a wok, heat oil, garlic and
chilli and stir-fry for 30 seconds. Add
chilli sauce and stir for 3 minutes.

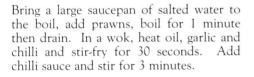

In a small bowl mix together cornflour
(cornstarch), stock, sugar and salt until
smooth, then stir into the wok. Bring to
the boil, stirring, then simmer until sauce
is thick. Add prawns and gently heat
through for about 2 minutes.

Serves 4.

MUSSELS WITH BEANS & CHILLI

3.25 kg (8 lb) mussels, scrubbed and rinsed
125 ml (4 fl oz/½ cup) vegetable oil
4 cloves garlic, finely chopped
2 hot red chillies, seeded if desired, finely
    chopped
½ green pepper (capsicum), seeded and
    chopped
3 spring onions, sliced
1 tablespoon cornflour (cornstarch) mixture, see
    page 10
4 tablespoons rice wine or dry sherry
3 tablespoons black bean paste
2 teaspoons ground ginger
1 tablespoon brown sugar
2 tablespoons hot chilli paste
3 tablespoons oyster sauce
750 ml (24 fl oz/3 cups) Chinese Chicken Stock,
    see page 29

Place mussels in a large saucepan, add 500 ml (16 fl oz/2 cups) water, cover and place over a high flame for about 5 minutes, shaking pan occasionally, or until the mussels have opened; this may have to be done in batches. Remove from heat, drain and discard any mussels which have not opened.

In a wok, heat oil, add garlic, chilli, green pepper (capsicum) and spring onions and stir-fry for 1 minute. In a bowl stir together remaining ingredients, stir into wok and bring to the boil, stirring. Simmer until lightly thickened.

Add mussels to wok and heat through for 5 minutes, occasionally shaking wok.

Serves 4 — 6.

SCALLOPS WITH BLACK BEANS

12 scallops on their half-shells
2 tablespoons peanut oil
2 cloves garlic, finely chopped
3 spring onions, finely chopped
1 fresh hot green chilli, seeded and chopped
3 tablespoons fermented salted black beans,
    soaked for 20 minutes, drained
2 tablespoons dark soy sauce
2 teaspoons brown sugar
3 tablespoons Chinese Chicken Stock, see
    page 29
2 teaspoons cornflour (cornstarch)

Place the scallops on their shells in a
steaming basket, place over a wok or
saucepan of boiling water, cover and cook
for 6 minutes.

Meanwhile, in a wok, heat oil, add garlic, spring onions, chilli and black beans
and stir-fry for 2 minutes, mashing the
beans. Stir in soy sauce and sugar for 1-2
minutes.

Blend stock with the cornflour
(cornstarch) until smooth. Stir into wok,
bring to the boil, stirring and simmer until
thickened. Keep warm.

Transfer scallops to a warmed serving
plate and spoon a little sauce over each.

Serves 4.

— SEA TREASURES STIR-FRY —

2 tablespoons cornflour (cornstarch)
1 egg white
185 g (6 oz) prepared raw prawns, see page 19
185 g (6 oz) prepared squid, see page 20
185 g (6 oz) shelled scallops, sliced
2 tablespoons peanut oil
1 medium carrot, thinly sliced
2 celery sticks, chopped
2.5 cm (1 in) piece fresh root ginger, peeled and
    finely chopped
3 cloves garlic, finely chopped
4 spring onions, finely chopped
125 ml (4 fl oz/½ cup) Chinese Chicken Stock,
    see page 29
1 teaspoon sea salt
1 tablespoon rice wine or dry sherry
1 teaspoon rice vinegar

In a bowl mix together cornflour (cornstarch) and egg white to make a light batter. Separately, dip prawns, squid and scallops into batter to coat evenly; allow excess batter to drain off. Reserve any remaining batter.

In a wok, heat oil, add prawns, scallops, squid, celery and carrot, fry for about 3 minutes, then drain on absorbent kitchen paper. Pour oil from wok, leaving just 1 tablespoonful. Stir in remaining ingredients and bring to the boil. Reduce heat so sauce simmers, add seafood and vegetables and stir gently for 2 minutes. If sauce is thin, stir in 1 teaspoon reserved batter to thicken.

Serves 4.

CANTONESE LOBSTER

1.5 kg (3 lb) lobster
2 tablespoons peanut oil
1 cm ($^1/_2$ in) piece fresh root ginger, peeled and
    grated
4 spring onions, coarsely chopped
1 teaspoon sea salt
185 ml (6 fl oz/$^3/_4$ cup) Chinese Chicken Stock,
    see page 29
2 tablespoons dark soy sauce
2 tablespoons rice wine or dry sherry

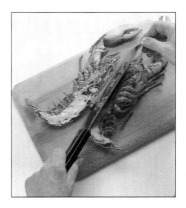

Insert the point of a large, heavy knife in the back of the head of the lobster, then move the knife towards the tail in a series of cutting movements, to split the lobster in half. Carefully remove the head sac and black intestinal thread; discard. Crack the claws.

In a wok, over a moderate heat, heat oil, add lobster pieces, cover and cook for 4 minutes. Remove and drain on absorbent kitchen paper. Pour oil from wok leaving just 1 tablespoonful. Stir remaining ingredients into the wok and bring to the boil. Return lobster pieces to wok, cover and simmer for 5 minutes. Transfer lobster to a warmed serving plate and pour sauce over.

Serves 4.

SQUID STIR-FRY

750 g (1 ½ lb) prepared squid, see page 20
3 tablespoons vegetable oil
4 spring onions, chopped
1 cm (½ in) fresh root ginger, peeled and finely
    chopped
1 carrot, cut into thin strips
5 tablespoons rice wine or dry sherry
185 ml (6 fl oz / ¾ cup) Chinese Chicken
    Stock, see page 29

Bring a large saucepan of lightly salted water to a rapid boil, add squid and boil for 3 minutes. Drain well.

In a wok, heat oil, add spring onions, garlic, ginger and carrot and stir-fry for 2 minutes. Stir in rice wine or dry sherry and cook for 1 minute. Pour in the stock, bring to the boil, and boil until thickened. Reduce heat, add squid and gently heat through.

Serves 4.

SQUID FLOWERS WITH PEPPERS

625 ml (20 fl oz/2 ½ cups) peanut oil
500 g (1 lb) prepared squid, see page 20
2 slices fresh root ginger, peeled and finely
    chopped
1 large green pepper (capsicum), seeded and cut
    into 2.5 cm (1 in) squares
1 teaspoon sea salt
1 tablespoon dark soy sauce
1 teaspoon rice vinegar
½ teaspoon brown sugar
ground black pepper
1 teaspoon sesame oil

In a wok, heat oil until smoking, add
squid and fry for 1 minute. Remove and
drain on absorbent kitchen paper. Pour
oil from wok, leaving just 1 tablespoonful.
Add ginger and green pepper (capsicum)
and stir-fry for 5 minutes until the pepper
(capsicum) begins to soften.

Stir in remaining ingredients except
sesame oil, bring to the boil, stirring,
reduce heat so sauce is simmering then
add squid and gently heat through.
Transfer to a warmed serving plate and
sprinkle with sesame oil.

Serves 4.

—— YELLOW RIVER CARP ——

1 kg (2 lb) carp, cleaned and scaled
2 teaspoons sea salt
2 tablespoons plain flour
2 tablespoons cornflour (cornstarch)
5-6 tablespoons cold water
625 ml (20 fl oz/2 ½ cups) peanut oil

Sauce:
1 tablespoon cornflour (cornstarch)
2 tablespoons brown sugar
4 tablespoons rice vinegar
1 tablespoon dark soy sauce
2 tablespoons rice wine or dry sherry
6 tablespoons water

Make 3 diagonal cuts in one direction, on
each side of fish. Make 3 more cuts on
each side, in the opposite direction, to
make a diamond pattern. Sprinkle inside
and out with salt. Mix together flour and
cornflour (cornstarch) then gradually stir
in enough water to make a light batter.
Pour and brush over fish until evenly
coated; allow excess to drain off. In a
wok, heat oil, gently lower in fish and fry
for 10 minutes until an even light golden
brown. Remove fish, drain on absorbent
kitchen paper then place on a warmed
serving plate and keep warm. Reserve oil.

To make the sauce, in a small saucepan,
heat 2 tablespoons of the reserved oil. In
a small bowl, mix together the cornflour
(cornstarch), sugar, vinegar, soy sauce, rice
wine or dry sherry and water. Pour into
the saucepan and cook over a medium
heat, stirring, until thickened. Pour over
fish.

Serves 4.

DRUNKEN FISH

2 tablespoons cornflour (cornstarch)
1 teaspoon sea salt
500 g (1 lb) haddock or other firm white fish
    fillets, thinly sliced
1 egg white, lightly beaten
625 ml (20 fl oz/2 ½ cups) vegetable oil
2 tablespoons peanut oil
12 dried black winter mushrooms

Sauce:
1 tablespoon cornflour (cornstarch) mixture, see
    page 10
60 ml (2 fl oz/¼ cup) Chinese Chicken Stock,
    see page 29
5 tablespoons rice wine or dry sherry
1 ½ teaspoons brown sugar

On a plate, mix together cornflour
(cornstarch) and salt, coat fish slices
evenly, shaking off any excess then dip fish
slices separately into the egg white to coat;
allow excess to drain off. In a wok, over a
medium flame, heat vegetable oil, add fish
and cook for 2 minutes on each side; the
fish should remain white. Remove, drain
on absorbent kitchen paper and keep
warm. In a medium saucepan, heat
peanut oil, add mushrooms and stir-fry
for 1 minute. Drain on absorbent kitchen
paper.

For the sauce, in a bowl, mix together ingredients, stir into wok, bring to the boil,
then simmer until sauce thickens. Gently
stir in fish to coat. To serve, place mushrooms on a serving dish, lay over the fish
slices and pour over the sauce.

Serves 4.

—— BAKED RED SNAPPER ——

1 kg (2 lb) red snapper, cleaned and scaled
1 teaspoon ground ginger
1 teaspoon sea salt
1 teaspoon ground black pepper
1 onion, sliced into rings
2.5 cm (1 in) piece fresh root ginger, peeled and
    finely chopped
1 tablespoon rice wine or dry sherry
1 tablespoon soy sauce
1 teaspoon brown sugar
1 ½ teaspoons salted (fermented) black beans,
    soaked for 20 minutes, drained
2 tablespoons peanut oil

Pre-heat oven to 180°C (350°F/Gas 4).

Wipe the fish; using a sharp knife, cut both sides diagonally in one direction then in the opposite direction to give a diamond pattern. In a small bowl, mix together ground ginger, salt and pepper. Rub into both sides of fish and sprinkle some inside. Cut a piece of cooking foil large enough to enclose fish completely; lay on a baking sheet. Lay a bed of onion and fresh ginger and place fish on top.

Mash black beans, rice wine or dry sherry, soy sauce and sugar together, then spread over fish. Heat oil until smoking and pour over the fish. Fold foil over fish and seal joins tightly. Bake for 20 minutes until the flesh flakes easily when tested with the back of a knife. Serve with the cooking juices spooned over.

Serves 4.

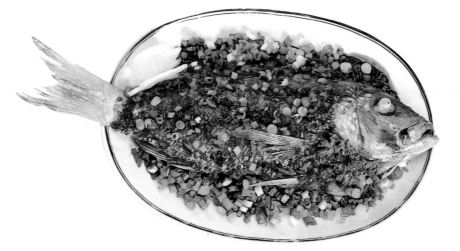

—FISH WITH SPRING ONIONS—

1 kg (2 lb) whole red snapper, sea bass or trout
   cleaned and scaled
1 ½ teaspoons sea salt
2 teaspoons sesame oil
1 cm (½ in) piece fresh root ginger, peeled and
   finely chopped
10 spring onions, coursely chopped
2 cloves garlic, finely chopped
½ teaspoon ground white pepper
5 teaspoons rice vinegar
3 teaspoons brown sugar
2 tablespoons dark soy sauce
250 ml (8 fl oz/1 cup) water

Sprinkle fish inside and out with salt.
Leave for 15 minutes, then rinse and dry
with absorbent kitchen paper.

In a wok, heat sesame oil, add garlic and
stir for 30 seconds.   Add fish and fry
gently for 2 minutes on each side, then
remove and drain on absorbent kitchen
paper and keep warm.

Add half the spring onions to the wok,
place fish on top, then cover with remaining spring onions. In a bowl mix together
remaining ingredients, pour over fish and
bring to the boil. Reduce heat so liquid
barely simmers, cover and cook for 45
minutes until the flesh flakes easily when
tested with the point of a knife.

Serves 4.

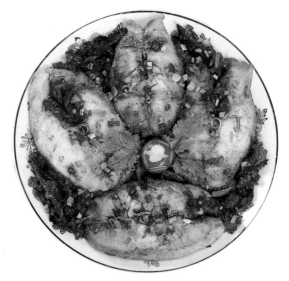

HUNAN FISH STEAKS

625 ml (20 fl oz/2 ¹/₂ cups) vegetable oil
4 cod steaks, 185 g (6 oz) each
4 spring onions, chopped, to serve
2 teaspoons sesame oil to serve

Sauce:
4 dried black winter mushrooms, soaked in hot
    water for 25 minutes
2 medium onions, finely chopped
3 slices fresh root ginger, peeled and finely
    chopped
2 cloves garlic, finely chopped
2 tablespoons Chinese radish pickle, chopped
3 dried red chillies
185 ml (6 fl oz/³/₄ cup) Chinese Chicken Stock,
    see page 29
3 tablespoons dark soy sauce
2 tablespoons brown sugar
2 teaspoons sea salt
4 tablespoons rice wine or dry sherry

In a wok, heat oil until just smoking. Add
fish steaks 2 at a time and deep fry for
1 ½ minutes each side; remove, drain on
absorbent kitchen paper and keep warm.
Reheat oil before adding the other steaks.

Pour oil from wok, leaving just 3
tablespoonsful. Stir in sauce ingredients
and boil, stirring until reduced by half.
Reduce heat so sauce is just simmering,
add fish steaks and heat through gently,
turning occasionally, for 5 minutes.
Transfer fish to a warmed serving plate,
pour over sauce, sprinkle with finely
chopped spring onions and sesame oil.

Serves 4.

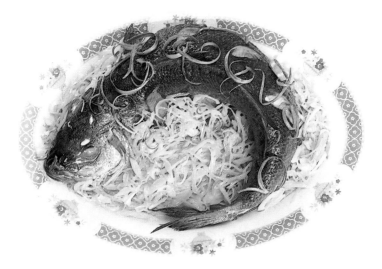

——— STEAMED SEA BASS ———

1 kg (2 lb) whole sea bass, snapper or trout,
    gutted and cleaned
2 tablespoons lemon juice
6 spring onions, shredded lengthways

Marinade:
1 tablespoon dark soy sauce
1 tablespoon cornflour (cornstarch)
1 tablespoon rice wine or dry sherry
$^1/_2$ teaspoon ground ginger
$^1/_2$ teaspoon ground black pepper

Sauce:
1 tablespoon Chinese Chicken Stock, page 29
2 tablespoons rice wine or dry sherry
1 teaspoon brown sugar
$^1/_2$ teaspoon sea salt
90 ml (3 fl oz/$^1/_3$ cup) peanut oil
2 small leeks, white part only, very finely sliced
1 cm ($^1/_2$ in) piece fresh root ginger, peeled and
    grated

With the point of a sharp knife, make
four diagonal cuts on each side of fish.
Sprinkle inside and out with lemon juice.
Place in a dish that will fit inside
a steamer. In a bowl, mix together
marinade ingredients. Pour over fish, turn
to coat with marinade; leave for 1 hour.
Place the dish in a steamer, cover, place
over a saucepan of boiling water and cook
20 minutes.

To make the sauce, in a saucepan, mix
together stock, rice wine or dry sherry
and salt, bring to a simmer and cook for 4
minutes. Remove from heat. In a wok,
heat oil, add leeks and ginger and gently
stir-fry for 2-3 minutes. Stir in contents of
saucepan; heat through. Transfer fish to a
warmed serving dish, pour over sauce and
sprinkle with shredded spring onions.

Serves 4.

– FISH STIR-FRY WITH GINGER –

60 g (2 oz/½ cup) cornflour (cornstarch)
½ teaspoon ground ginger
1 teaspoon ground sea salt
750 g (1 ½ lb) haddock or other firm white fish
    fillets, skinned and cubed
3 tablespoons peanut oil
2.5 cm (1 in) piece fresh root ginger, peeled and
    finely chopped
4 spring onions, thinly sliced
1 tablespoon ChingKiang vinegar or red wine
    vinegar
2 tablespoons rice wine or dry sherry
3 tablespoons dark soy sauce
1 teaspoon sugar
3 tablespoons fresh orange juice

In a bowl, mix together cornflour (cornstarch), ground ginger and salt, add fish in batches to coat evenly.

In a wok, heat oil. Add fish and fry for 4 minutes, occasionally turning gently, until evenly browned. In a bowl, mix together remaining ingredients, stir into wok, reduce the heat so the liquid just simmers, cover and cook for 4 minutes.

Serves 4.

SNAPPER IN HOT BEAN SAUCE

250 ml (8 fl oz/1 cup) peanut oil
1 kg (2 lb) red snapper, porgy or trout
4 cloves garlic, finely chopped
2 tablespoons hot bean sauce
185 ml (6 fl oz/³/₄ cup) Chinese Chicken Stock,
    see page 29
1 tablespoon red wine vinegar
1 tablespoon rice wine or dry sherry
3 slices fresh root ginger, peeled and finely
    chopped
1 tablespoon dark soy sauce
¹/₂ teaspoon sea salt
1 ¹/₂ teaspoons cornflour (cornstarch)
3 spring onions, finely chopped, to garnish

In a wok heat oil. Add fish and fry for 4 minutes on each side until just beginning to brown. Remove, drain on absorbent paper and keep warm. Pour oil from wok, leaving just 2 tablespoonsful. Add garlic, stir-fry for 30 seconds, then add hot bean sauce and stir for a further 30 seconds. Stir in remaining ingredients, except spring onions, and bring to the boil, stirring. Reduce heat, add fish, bring to just on simmering point, cover and cook for 25 minutes. Check frequently to make sure sauce is not drying out; if necessary stir in a little water.

Transfer fish to a warmed plate, pour over sauce and garnish with finely chopped spring onions.

Serves 4.

— SWEET AND SOUR FISH —

½ teaspoon sea salt
2 tablespoons cornflour (cornstarch)
4 haddock fillets, 185 g (6 oz) each
1 egg white, beaten
625 ml (20 fl oz/2 ½ cups) vegetable oil

Sauce:
1 tablespoon brown sugar
2 tablespoons rice vinegar
1 tablespoon Chinese Chicken Stock, see page 29
1 tablespoon chilli sauce
2 tablespoons fresh orange juice
1 tablespoon cornflour (cornstarch) mixture, see
    page 10

On a plate, mix together salt and cornflour (cornstarch) then coat fish evenly, shaking off any excess. Dip each fillet in egg white.

In a wok, heat oil. Add fish and deep-fry for 5 minutes until golden. Drain on absorbent kitchen paper and keep warm.

In a medium saucepan, mix together sauce ingredients, bring to the boil, stirring, then simmer for 3 minutes. Transfer the fish to a warmed serving plate and pour over sauce.

Serves 4.

CHICKEN IN BLACK BEAN SAUCE

250 ml (8 fl oz/1 cup) peanut oil
500 g (1 lb) boned chicken breast, cubed
10 button mushrooms, halved
½ red pepper (capsicum), seeded and diced
½ green pepper (capsicum), seeded and diced
4 spring onions, finely chopped
2 carrots, thinly sliced
2 tablespoons dried black beans, washed
1 cm (½ in) piece fresh root ginger, peeled and
    grated
1 clove garlic, finely chopped
2 tablespoons rice wine or dry sherry
250 ml (8 fl oz/1 cup) Chinese Vegetable Stock,
    see page 30
1 tablespoon light soy sauce
2 tablespoons cornflour (cornstarch) mixture, see
    page 10

In a wok, heat oil until smoking, add
chicken cubes and deep-fry for 2 minutes.
Using a slotted spoon, lift chicken from
oil and drain on absorbent kitchen paper.
Pour oil from wok, leaving just 2
tablespoonsful.

Add mushrooms to wok and stir-fry for 1
minute. Add red and green peppers (capsicums) and spring onions and carrots,
stir-fry for 3 minutes. In a bowl, mash
black beans with ginger, garlic and rice
wine or dry sherry, stir into wok then stir
in stock and soy sauce. Cook for another
2 minutes. Stir in cornflour (cornstarch)
mixture and bring to the boil, stirring.
Stir in chicken and heat through gently.

Serves 4.

MANDARIN CHICKEN

500 g (1 lb) boned chicken breasts, diced
500 ml (16 fl oz/2 cups) peanut oil
2 dried red chillies, chopped
1 teaspoon Szechuan peppercorns
90 g (3 oz) unsalted peanuts, skinned
4 slices fresh root ginger, peeled and finely
    chopped
2 cloves garlic, thinly sliced
3 spring onions, finely chopped
155 ml (5 fl oz/²/₃ cup) Chinese Chicken Stock,
    see page 29
1 tablespoon light soy sauce
1 teaspoon brown sugar
1 teaspoon rice vinegar
1 ½ teaspoons cornflour (cornstarch)

Marinade:
½ teaspoon sea salt
1 tablespoon light soy sauce
1 tablespoon rice wine or dry sherry
1 ½ teaspoons cornflour (cornstarch)

In a bowl, mix together marinade ingredients. Stir in chicken to coat evenly,
then leave for 1 hour.

In a wok, heat oil until smoking, add
chillies and peppercorns in a wire strainer
and deep fry for 1 minute. Drain on
absorbent kitchen paper and reserve.
Reheat oil and deep fry chicken for 5
minutes until firm, white and cooked
through. At last moment, add peanuts in a
small metal basket and fry for a few
seconds until brown; drain on absorbent
kitchen paper.

Using a slotted spoon lift chicken from oil and drain on absorbent kitchen paper. Pour oil from wok, leaving just 3 tablespoonsful.

Add ginger, garlic and spring onions to wok and stir-fry for 30 seconds. Add chicken, chillies and peppercorns and stir fry for 3 minutes.

In a bowl mix together stock, soy sauce, sugar, rice vinegar and cornflour (cornstarch); stir into the wok with the peanuts. Bring to the boil, stirring, then reduce heat and cook for 1-2 minutes.

Serves 4.

CRISPY-SKIN CHICKEN

1.5 kg (3 lb) chicken
salt
1 tablespoon golden syrup
4 tablespoons plus 1 teaspoon sea salt
3 ¹/₂ teaspoons Chinese five-spice powder
2 tablespoons rice vinegar
925 ml (30 fl oz/3 ³/₄ cups) vegetable oil

Bring a large saucepan of salted water to the boil. Lower in chicken, return to the boil, then remove pan from heat, cover tightly and leave the chicken in the water for 30 minutes.

Drain chicken, dry with absorbent kitchen paper and leave in a cold dry place for at least 12 hours. In a small bowl, mix together golden syrup, 1 teaspoon salt, ¹/₂ teaspoon five-spice powder and rice vinegar. Brush over chicken and leave in the refrigerator for 20 minutes. Repeat until all the coating is used. Refrigerate the chicken for at least 4 hours to allow the coating to dry thoroughly on the skin.

Split chicken in half, through the breast. In a wok, heat oil, add chicken halves and deep-fry for 5 minutes until golden brown. Lift chicken from oil and drain on absorbent kitchen paper. Cut into bite-sized pieces. In a small saucepan over a low heat, stir together remaining sea salt and remaining five spice powder for 2 minutes. Sprinkle over chicken.

Serves 4.

FIVE-SPICE CHICKEN

500 ml (16 fl oz/2 cups) peanut oil
1 tablespoon dark soy sauce
1 tablespoon brandy
½ teaspoon Chinese five-spice powder
½ teaspoon brown sugar
1 cm (½ in) piece fresh root ginger, peeled and
    finely chopped
2 spring onions, finely chopped
2 cloves garlic, finely chopped
500 g (1 lb) boned chicken breast, cubed
1 large egg, beaten
60 g (2 oz/½ cup) cornflour (cornstarch)

In a large bowl, mix together 2 tablespoons peanut oil, soy sauce, brandy, five-spice powder, sugar, ginger, onions and garlic. Stir in chicken cubes to coat evenly. Leave for at least 1 hour. Stir in beaten egg. Put cornflour (cornstarch) on a plate, roll each chicken cube in cornflour (cornstarch) until evenly coated.

In a wok, heat remaining oil over a moderate heat, add chicken and deep-fry for 4 minutes. Increase heat and fry for 2 minutes until golden and cooked through. Using a slotted spoon, lift chicken from oil and drain on absorbent kitchen paper.

Serves 4.

STEAMED CHICKEN WITH MUSHROOMS

2 teaspoons rice wine or dry sherry
2 tablespoons light soy sauce
½ teaspoon sea salt
1 teaspoon sugar
2 tablespoons Chinese Chicken Stock, see
    page 29
440 g (14 oz) can straw mushrooms, drained,
    liquid reserved
500 g (1 lb) boned chicken breasts, cubed
2 slices fresh root ginger, peeled and chopped
3 spring onions, coarsely chopped

In a bowl, mix together rice wine or dry sherry, soy sauce, salt, sugar, stock and reserved mushroom liquid.

Place chicken in a heatproof casserole with mushrooms, pour over contents of bowl then sprinkle with ginger and spring onions; cover casserole. Place in a steamer, cover and cook for 10 minutes until chicken is firm and tender. Remove dish from steamer and pour off cooking liquid into a wok. Bring to the boil, simmer for 2-3 minutes, then pour over the chicken.

Serves 6.

DUCK IN LEMON JUICE

2 tablespoons water
1 tablespoon rice wine or dry sherry
2.5 cm (1 in) piece fresh root ginger, peeled and
    grated
3 spring onions, finely chopped
1 teaspoon sea salt
500 g (1 lb) boned duck breasts, cut into finger
    sized pieces
2 eggs, well beaten
125 g (4 oz/1 cup) cornflour (cornstarch)
750 ml (24 fl oz/3 cups) peanut oil
1 teaspoon sesame oil

Sauce:
375 ml (12 fl oz/1 ½ cups) Chinese Chicken
    Stock, see page 29
3 tablespoons rice wine or dry sherry
4 tablespoons lemon juice
1 teaspoon brown sugar

In a bowl mix together, water, rice wine or
dry sherry, ginger, spring onions and salt.
Stir in duck to coat evenly then leave for
2 hours. Lift duck from bowl then dip
each piece in beaten egg, allowing excess
to drain off. Roll duck pieces in cornflour
(cornstarch) to coat lightly and evenly.

In a wok, heat peanut oil to smoking
point, add duck and deep-fry for 3
minutes until golden. Using a slotted
spoon remove duck from oil and drain on
absorbent kitchen paper. Place duck in a
flameproof casserole. In a small bowl,
mix together sauce ingredients; stir into
casserole. Bring to the boil, stirring
constantly, then simmer for 10-15 minutes
until duck is tender and sauce very thick.
Serve sprinkled with sesame oil

Serves 4.

PEKING DUCK

1.75 kg (4 lb) oven-ready duck
1 tablespoon honey
3 tablespoons dark soy sauce
1 tablespoon sesame oil
edible red food colouring, if desired
2 tablespoons water

Pancakes:
500 g (1 lb/4 cups) plain (all-purpose) flour
250 ml (8 fl oz/1 cup) boiling water
90 ml (3 fl oz/^{1}/3 cup) cold water
1 teaspoon sesame oil

To serve:
hoisin sauce
6 spring onions, cut into long shreds
^{1}/2 cucumber, cut into long shreds

Place the duck in a colander in the sink. Pour over boiling water; repeat twice. Hang duck overnight in a cold airy place, or place on a rack in the refrigerator. Next morning, in a small bowl, mix together honey, soy sauce, sesame oil and colouring, if used. Place duck on a rack in a roasting tin, making sure the neck opening is closed. Brush evenly with honey mixture and leave for at least 1 hour.

Pre-heat oven to 200C (400F/Gas 6).

Stir water into remaining honey mixture and pour through the vent, into the duck. With a meat skewer or wooden cocktail sticks, secure vent. Roast duck, 1 ½ hours, until juices run clear. Remove duck from oven and leave in a warm place for 10 minutes before carving.

Meanwhile, make the pancakes. Sift flour into a bowl and gradually stir in boiling water; mix well. Stir in cold water to form a ball. On a floured surface, knead until smooth. Return to bowl, cover with a damp cloth and leave for 15 minutes.

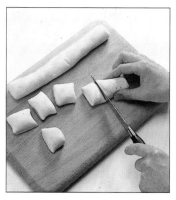

Divide dough in half on a lightly floured surface, roll each half to a long roll 5 cm (2 in) in diameter. Cut into 2.5 cm (1 in) lengths. Flatten each piece with the palm of the hand. Lightly brush tops with sesame oil and place two pieces together, oiled-sides facing. Roll out each pair to 15 cm (6 in) pancakes. Place a dry, non-stick frying pan over a moderate heat and fry each pancake for 20-30 seconds until beginning to bubble. Turn over pancake and cook for a further 10-15 seconds until lightly browned.

Remove from pan and carefully separate the top and bottom. Keep warm, interleaved with greaseproof paper.

Serve the carved duck on a warm plate with the stack of pancakes, and with hoisin sauce, spring onions and cucumber in separate bowls.

Serves 4.

— SZECHUAN CRISPY DUCK —

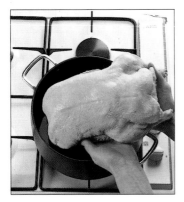

1.2 litres (40 fl oz/5 cups) Chinese Chicken
   Stock, see page 29
1 cm ($^1/_2$ in) piece fresh root ginger, peeled and
   sliced
3 tablespoons rice wine or dry sherry
1 tablespoon Szechuan peppercorns, lightly
   crushed
2 teaspoons sea salt
8 tablespoons dark soy sauce
8 tablespoons brown sugar
4 pieces star anise
1.5 kg (3 lb) duck
925 ml (30 fl oz/3 $^3/_4$ cups) peanut oil

In a large saucepan, mix together all ingredients except duck and oil and bring to
the boil.

Lower duck into liquid, return to the boil,
then reduce the heat so the liquid is just
simmering. Cook duck for 2 ½-3 hours.
Drain duck, cool and cut in half through
the breast bone. In a wok, heat oil until smoking, add duck halves and deep-
fry for 5 minutes until crisp and golden
brown. Drain on absorbent kitchen paper
and serve as Peking Duck, see page 72.

Serves 4.

STIR-FRIED DUCK WITH LEEKS

4 tablespoons vegetable oil
2 leeks, thinly shredded
1 red pepper (capsicum), seeded and sliced
1 cm (½ in) piece fresh root ginger, peeled and
    thinly sliced
3 cloves garlic, finely chopped
2 tablespoons black bean paste
500 g (1 lb) cooked boned duck, cut into strips
60 ml (2 fl oz/¼ cup) Chinese Stock, see page 29
2 tablespoons light soy sauce
2 tablespoons rice vinegar
2 teaspoons brown sugar
2 teaspoons chilli sauce

In a wok, heat oil until just smoking. Add leeks, pepper (capsicum), ginger and garlic. Stir-fry briefly to coat with oil, then stir in black bean paste and stir-fry for 5 minutes until vegetables begin to soften.

Add duck and remaining ingredients and stir-fry for 2-3 minutes until duck is heated through.

Serves 4.

– DUCK WITH GREEN PEPPERS –

1 egg-white
3 tablespoons cornflour (cornstarch)
sea salt
500 g (1 lb) boned duck breasts, cubed
625 ml (20 fl oz/2 ½ cups) peanut oil
2 green peppers, seeded and cut into 2.5 cm
    (1 in) squares
2 tablespoons light soy sauce
3 teaspoons rice wine or dry sherry
1 teaspoon brown sugar
125 ml (4 fl oz/½ cup) Chinese Chicken Stock,
    see page 29
1 teaspoon sesame oil
white pepper

In a bowl, whisk together egg white,
cornflour (cornstarch) and 1 teaspoon salt.
Stir in duck cubes to mix thoroughly.
Leave for 20 minutes.

In a wok, heat peanut oil until very hot.
Add duck and deep-fry for about 4
minutes, until crisp. Remove and drain
on absorbent kitchen paper. Add peppers
to wok and deep-fry for 2 minutes then
drain on absorbent kitchen paper. Pour
oil from wok, leaving 2 tablespoonsful.
Add soy sauce, rice wine or dry sherry,
sugar, stock, sesame oil, and salt and
pepper to taste. Boil then add cooked
duck, peppers and gently heat through.

Serves 4.

— LAMB WITH CORIANDER —

500 g (1 lb) lamb fillet, cut into thin strips
1 tablespoon cornflour (cornstarch)
1 teaspoon granulated sugar
1 teaspoon sesame oil
2 tablespoons peanut oil
185 g (6 oz) broccoli florets, sliced
3 dried black winter mushrooms, soaked in hot
    water for 25 minutes, drained
2 spring onions, chopped
1 clove garlic, finely chopped
2 teaspoons rice wine or dry sherry
1 tablespoon dark soy sauce
1 tablespoon finely chopped fresh coriander

Place lamb in a dish. In a bowl, mix together cornflour (cornstarch), sugar and sesame oil and spoon over the lamb; stir to well-coat lamb. Leave for 30 minutes.

In a wok, heat peanut oil, add lamb and stir-fry for 2 minutes. Remove lamb from wok and keep warm. Add broccoli, mushrooms, spring onions and garlic and stir-fry for about 5 minutes until broccoli is just tender. Stir in rice wine or dry sherry, soy sauce, lamb and coriander. Stir over a very high heat for 1 minute.

Serves 4.

LAMB CHOPS MONGOLIAN STYLE

1 tablespoon hoisin sauce
1 tablespoon dark soy sauce
2 cloves garlic, finely chopped
1 teaspoon sea salt
¼ teaspoon ground white pepper
4 lamb chops, 185-250 g (6-8 oz) each
2 tablespoons peanut oil
2 medium onions, sliced
60 ml (2 fl oz/¼ cup) Vegetable Stock, see
   page 30

Sauce:
1 fresh hot red chilli, seeded and sliced
1 hot fresh green chilli, seeded and sliced
½ teaspoon sea salt
1 tablespoon lemon juice
1 teaspoon brown sugar
2 tablespoons peanut oil

In a bowl, mix together hoisin sauce, soy
sauce, garlic, salt and pepper. Coat chops
with mixture and leave for 1 hour.

In a wok, heat oil until smoking, add
onions and fry for 2 minutes until
transparent. Reduce heat, add chops and
cook for about 5 minutes each side. Add
stock, cover and gently cook for 5
minutes. In a bowl, mix together all sauce
ingredients, pour into a small saucepan
and heat gently. Transfer chops to a
warmed serving plate and pour over
sauce.

Serves 4.

—— HUNAN LAMB STIR-FRY ——

1 egg white lightly beaten
2 tablespoons cornflour (cornstarch)
ground white pepper to taste
500 g (1 lb) lamb fillet, thinly sliced
625 ml (20 fl oz/2 ½ cups) vegetable oil
3 slices fresh root ginger, peeled and finely
    chopped
90 g (3 oz) canned bamboo shoots, drained and
    chopped
1 small red pepper (capsicum), seeded and cut
    into thin strips
3 spring onions, finely chopped
60 g (2 oz) cucumber, cut into strips
2 teaspoons rice wine or dry sherry

In a small bowl, mix together egg white,
cornflour (cornstarch), salt and pepper.
Stir lamb slices in mixture to evenly coat.
Leave for 30 minutes.

In a wok, heat oil, add lamb in batches,
keeping slices separate, and deep-fry lamb
for 2 minutes. Using a slotted spoon, lift
lamb from oil and drain on absorbent
kitchen paper. Pour oil from wok, leaving just 2 tablespoonsful. Add ginger,
bamboo shoots, pepper (capsicum), spring
onions and cucumber and stir-fry for 4
minutes. Add lamb and toss over a high
heat for 1 minute. Stir in rice wine or dry
sherry.

Serves 4.

—— LAMB IN GARLIC SAUCE ——

500 g (1 lb) lamb tenderloin, very thinly sliced
3 tablepoons dark soy sauce
5 tablespoons peanut oil
1 tablespoon rice wine or dry sherry
½ teaspoon sea salt
2 cloves garlic, chopped
8 spring onions, chopped
1 tablespoon rice vinegar
½ teaspoon ground Szechuan pepper
2 tablespoons sesame oil

Lay lamb in a shallow dish. In a bowl, mix together 1 tablespoon soy sauce, 2 tablespoons peanut oil, the rice wine or dry sherry, salt and Szechuan pepper. Pour over lamb, turn to coat then leave for 30 minutes.

In a wok, heat remaining peanut oil until smoking, add garlic and lamb. Stir-fry for 2 minutes until lamb just changes colour; remove from wok. Pour oil from wok, leaving just 1 tablespoonful. Add spring onions and stir-fry for 2 minutes. Add remaining soy sauce and the vinegar. Continue stir-frying for another minute then add the lamb slices and sesame oil. Stir-fry for 1 minute making sure lamb and sauce are thoroughly mixed.

Serves 4.

- LAMB WITH SPRING ONIONS -

1 egg white
60 g (2 oz / ½ cup) cornflour (cornstarch)
1 teaspoon sea salt
1 tablespoon rice wine or dry sherry
500 g (1 lb) lamb fillet, cut into strips
315 ml (10 fl oz/1 ¼ cups) vegetable oil
10 spring onions, chopped
1 cm (½ in) piece fresh root ginger, peeled and finely
    chopped
2 cloves garlic, finely chopped
1 teaspoon brown sugar
2 teaspoons dark soy sauce
¼ teaspoon ground white pepper
1 teaspoon sesame oil to serve

In a bowl, mix together egg white,
cornflour (cornstarch), ½ teaspoon salt,
and rice wine or dry sherry. Stir in lamb
strips to coat thoroughly.

In a wok, heat oil until smoking, add lamb
in small batches, keeping strips separate
and fry for 2 minutes. Using a slotted
spoon remove lamb from wok, drain
on absorbent kitchen paper and keep
warm. Pour oil from wok, leaving just 1
tablespoonful.   Stir in spring onions,
ginger, garlic, remaining salt, sugar, soy
sauce and pepper mixture. Add lamb and
heat through gently. Serve sprinkled with
sesame oil.

Serves 4.

— CHINESE BARBECUED LAMB —

2 small eggs, beaten
90 g (3 oz/³/₄ cup) plain (all purpose) flour
1 teaspoon sea salt
¹/₂ teaspoon ground black pepper
1 teaspoon ground Szechuan pepper
4 spring onions, finely chopped
2 medium tomatoes, seeded and finely chopped
500 g (1 lb) lamb fillet, cut into cubes
4 teaspoons sesame seeds

In a bowl, mix together all ingredients, except lamb and sesame seeds. Stir in lamb to coat, cover and leave in a cool place for 4 hours.

Pre-heat grill or barbecue. Spread sesame seeds out on a plate. Roll lamb cubes in sesame seeds to coat evenly. Thread cubes on to skewers and sprinkle on any remaining sesame seeds. Grill or barbecue for 4-5 minutes, turning frequently, until tender.

Serves 4.

PORK WITH MANGE TOUT (SNOW PEAS)

4 pork chops, each weighing 185-250 g (6-8 oz),
   boned and sliced thinly lengthwise.
1 teaspoon dark soy sauce
1 tablespoon yellow bean paste
2 tablespoons peanut oil
2 tablespoons Chinese rose wine or sweet sherry
2 carrots, sliced
250 g (8 oz) mange tout (snow peas)
2 cloves garlic, finely chopped
2.5 cm (1 in) piece fresh root ginger, peeled and
   finely chopped

Place pork in a dish. In a small bowl, mix together soy sauce, bean paste, 1 tablespoon peanut oil and rose wine or sweet sherry, then pour over pork. Turn slices to coat well and leave to marinate for 1 hour. Drain and reserve marinade. Bring a saucepan of water to a rapid boil, add carrots, mange tout (snow peas) and boil for 1 minute. Drain and refresh under cold running water.

In a wok, heat 1 tablespoon peanut oil, fry garlic and ginger for 2-3 minutes until browned, then discard. Add pork to wok and stir-fry for 3-4 minutes until it changes colour. Add carrot and mange tout (snow peas) and stir-fry for 3 minutes, then pour in reserved marinade. Heat through for 2 minutes.

Serves 4.

CHAI SUI ROAST PORK

500 g (1 lb) pork fillet
2 tablespoons rice wine or dry sherry
3 tablespoons brown sugar
3 tablespoons peanut oil
1 tablespoon yellow bean paste
2 tablespoons dark soy sauce
2 tablespoons red fermented tofu

In a bowl, mix together all ingredients, except pork. Spoon over pork and leave at room temperature for 1 hour.

Pre-heat oven to 200°C (400°F/Gas 6).Put joint on a rack in a roasting tin and roast for 15-20 minutes until juices run clear and outside is richly coloured.

Serves 4.

─── PORK WITH NOODLES ───

250 g (8 oz) dried egg noodles
3 tablespoons peanut oil
1 medium Spanish onion, finely chopped
2 cloves garlic, finely chopped
2 slices fresh root ginger, peeled and finely chopped
2 teaspoons yellow bean paste
1 tablespoon light soy sauce
500 g (1 lb) pork tenderloin, minced
3 tablespoons Chicken Stock, see page 29
1 tablespoon cornflour (cornstarch) mixture, see
  page 12
185 g (6 oz) cucumber, cut into thin sticks, to garnish
spring onions, finely chopped, to garnish

Cook noodles in boiling water until just tender, drain well.   Meanwhile, in a wok, heat oil, add Spanish onion, garlic and ginger and stir-fry for 2 minutes.   Stir in bean paste and soy sauce; cook for a further minute.   Stir in pork, reduce heat and cook gently for 10 minutes until lightly coloured. Stir in stock and simmer for 5 minutes.   Stir in cornflour (cornstarch) mixture and simmer until thickened.

To serve, place noodles on a warmed serving dish, pour over pork and garnish with cucumber and spring onions.

Serves 4.

— SWEET AND SOUR PORK —

2 teaspoons rice wine or dry sherry
1 large egg, beaten
125 g (4 oz/1 cup)) cornflour (cornstarch)
500g (1 lb) belly pork, cubed
625 ml (20 fl oz/2 ½ cups) peanut oil
3 spring onions, thinly sliced
90 g (3 oz) can bamboo shoots, drained and
    thinly sliced
1 green pepper (capsicum), seeded and thinly
    sliced
½ teaspoon sea salt
2 cloves garlic, finely chopped
1 teaspoon sesame oil

Sauce:
2 tablespoons brown sugar
1 tablespoon vegetable oil
3 tablespoons malt vinegar
1 teaspoon cornflour (cornstarch)
sea salt and white pepper

In a bowl, mix together salt, rice wine or
dry sherry and egg.   Stir in pork to
evenly coat. Remove the pork and roll in
cornflour (cornstarch) to coat evenly. In a
wok, heat peanut oil until smoking and
deep-fry pork for about 5 minutes until
crisp and well cooked. Using a slotted
spoon, lift pork from oil and drain on
absorbent kitchen paper.

Pour oil from wok, leaving just 2
tablespoonsful. Add vegetables and garlic
and stir-fry for 3 minutes. Stir in pork
and mix thoroughly. To make the sauce,
in a saucepan, stir together all ingredients
and place over a moderate heat for 4
minutes, stirring continuously until hot
and well blended. Pour over pork and
briefly heat together.   Sprinkle with
sesame oil and serve.

Serves 4.

SZECHUAN PORK

3 tablespoons vegetable oil
185 g (6 oz) Szechuan preserved cabbage, soaked
    for 1 hour, drained and shredded
500 g (1 lb) pork tenderloin, very thinly sliced
3 spring onions, finely chopped
3 slices fresh root ginger, peeled and finely
    chopped
1 fresh red chilli, seeded and very finely sliced
1 red pepper (capsicum), seeded and cut into
    strips
1 tablespoon light soy sauce
2 tablespoons rice wine or dry sherry
½ teaspoon brown sugar

In a wok, heat oil, add cabbage and pork and stir-fry for 2 minutes until pork changes colour. Stir in spring onions, ginger, chilli and pepper (capsicum).

In a small bowl, mix together remaining ingredients. Stir into wok and cook for 2 minutes.

Serves 4.

—— BARBECUED PORK ——

750 g (1 ½ lb) pork loin, cut into long strips
125 g (4 oz/²/₃ cup) brown sugar
3 tablespoons boiling water
1 tablespoon dark soy sauce
1 tablespoon oyster sauce
2 tablespoons rice wine or dry sherry
1 teaspoon sesame oil
½ teaspoon sea salt
½ teaspoon edible red food colouring, if desired
Chinese shredded lettuce, to serve

Place pork in a medium bowl. In a small bowl, stir together sugar and boiling water until sugar dissolves, then stir in remaining ingredients. Cool slightly, then pour over pork, turning pork several times to coat evenly. Leave for 8 hours turning the pork several times. Lift pork from marinade, allowing excess to drain off, reserve.

Pre-heat barbecue or grill.

Thread meat onto meat skewers and barbecue or grill for about 8 minutes until crisp and cooked, basting several times with reserved marinade.

To serve, remove the pork from the skewers, cut into bite-sized pieces and serve on a bed of shredded Chinese lettuce.

Serves 4-6.

– PORK WITH CASHEW NUTS –

1 teaspoon rice wine or dry sherry
$^1/_2$ teaspoon sea salt
1 teaspoon sugar
2 teaspoons cornflour (cornstarch)
500 g (1 lb) pork tenderloin, cubed
625 ml (20 fl oz/2 $^1/_2$ cups) peanut oil
125 g (4 oz) cashew nuts
3 cloves garlic, finely chopped
2 spring onions, coarsely chopped
$^1/_2$ red pepper (capsicum), seeded and diced
$^1/_2$ green pepper (capsicum), seeded and diced
4 dried winter mushrooms, soaked in hot water
for 25 minutes, drained

Sauce:
1 teaspoon light soy sauce
$^1/_2$ teaspoon sea salt
$^1/_4$ teaspoon ground white pepper
1 teaspoon cornflour (cornstarch)
75 ml (2 $^1/_2$ fl oz/$^1/_3$ cup) Chinese Chicken
Stock, see page 29

In a bowl, mix together, rice wine or dry sherry, salt, sugar and cornflour (cornstarch). Stir in pork to coat evenly. Leave for 30 minutes.In a wok, heat oil, until very hot, add pork and deep-fry for 3-4 minutes until cooked through. Using a slotted spoon, lift out pork and drain on absorbent kitchen paper.

Place nuts in a small wire basket, lower into oil and deep-fry for a few seconds until lightly coloured. Drain on absorbent kitchen paper. Pour oil from wok, leaving just 1 tablespoonful. Add garlic, fry briefly then add all the vegetables. Continue cooking for 3-4 minutes. In a bowl, mix together sauce ingredients, stir into wok and simmer until thickened. Stir in pork and heat through gently.

Serves 4.

—— CHINESE ROAST BEEF ——

1.5 kg (3 lb) sirloin of beef
2 cloves garlic, thinly sliced
½ teaspoon Chinese five-spice powder
sea salt
¼ teaspoon ground black pepper
8 potatoes, quartered
12 dried black winter mushrooms, soaked in hot
**   water for 25 minutes, drained**

Pre-heat oven to 200°C (400°F/Gas 6).

With the point of a sharp knife, cut small incisions in the beef and insert thin slices of garlic. In a bowl, mix together five-spice powder, 1 teaspoon salt and pepper, then rub into beef. Place in a baking dish and cook for 45 minutes, turning beef and basting at least once.

Boil potatoes in salted water for 10 minutes. Drain well; when cool enough to handle, slice. Add to baking dish with mushrooms and cook for a further 15 minutes.

Serves 8.

– BOILED BEEF WITH CHILLIES –

500 g (1 lb) rump steak, cut into paper thin
    slices
8 lettuce leaves, diced
½ teaspoon ground Szechuan pepper
1 clove garlic, finely chopped

Sauce:
2 tablespoons peanut oil
4 dried red chillies, crushed
1 teaspoon ground Szechuan pepper
1 tablespoon fermented black beans
4 spring onions, coarsely chopped
2 cloves garlic, crushed
1 cm (½ in) piece fresh root ginger, peeled and
    finely chopped
1 tablespoon hot bean paste
125 ml (4 fl oz/½ cup water)

To make the sauce, in a wok, heat oil
and briskly fry chillies and pepper for 30
seconds, then add black beans and cook
for a further 30 seconds. Add spring
onions, garlic, ginger and bean paste, and
continue to fry for 5-6 minutes. Stir in
water and bring to the boil, then remove
from the heat.

To prepare the beef, bring a large
saucepan of water to a rapid boil. Add
beef and boil for 2 minutes until it just
changes colour. Drain well. Re-heat
sauce in the wok, add beef, stir for 3
minutes, then add the lettuce. Serve
immediately sprinkled with Szechuan
pepper and finely chopped garlic.

Serves 4.

— BEEF WITH GREEN PEPPERS —

4 tablespoons peanut oil
2.5 cm (1 in) piece fresh root ginger, peeled and
    sliced thinly
500 g (1 lb) fillet steak, very thinly sliced
2 green peppers (capsicums), seeded and cut into
    small squares

Sauce:
60 ml (2 fl oz/¼ cup) Chinese Vegetable Stock,
    see page 30
1 tablespoon dark soy sauce
1 teaspoon sesame oil
1 hot fresh red chilli, finely chopped
2 tablespoons Chinese rose wine
2 tablespoons cornflour (cornstarch) mixture, see
    page 10

In a wok, heat oil, add ginger and fry for
1 minute. Add beef and quickly stir-fry
for 2 minutes until just changing colour.
Stir in peppers (capsicums) and fry for 5
minutes.

In a small bowl, mix together sauce ingredients. Stir into beef mixture until
lightly thickened.

Serves 4.

BEEF WITH CHOI SUM

500 g (1 lb) rump steak, trimmed and cut into
    thin strips
125 ml (4 fl oz/½ cup) peanut oil
250 g (8 oz) choi sum or young spinach, washed
    and dried
sea salt
1 teaspoon grated fresh root ginger
2 cloves garlic, finely chopped
4 spring onions, coarsely chopped
2 teaspoons shrimp paste
1 teaspoon rice wine or dry sherry
½ teaspoon cornflour (cornstarch) mixture, see
    page 10
60 ml (2 fl oz/¼ cup) Chinese Chicken Stock,
    see page 29
1 teaspoon sesame oil

Marinade:
1 teaspoon dark soy sauce
1 teaspoon anchovy essence
1 tablespoon peanut oil
1 tablespoon cornflour (cornstarch)
1 teaspoon water

In a small bowl, mix together marinade
ingredients. Stir in steak to coat evenly.
Leave for 1 hour.In a wok, heat oil and fry
choi sum or spinach over a high heat for 2
minutes, sprinkle with salt and transfer to
a warmed serving plate. Keep warm.

Reheat wok and stir-fry beef for 2 minutes
until it just changes colour, then remove.
Add ginger, garlic and spring onions
and fry until tender, about 5 minutes.
In a small bowl, mix together shrimp
paste, rice wine or dry sherry, cornflour
(cornstarch) mixture and stock. Pour into
wok and bring to the boil, stirring. Stir in
beef to heat through. Arrange beef and
choi sum or spinach attractively on the
plate and sprinkle with sesame oil.

Serves 4.

GREEN BEAN STIR-FRY

4 teaspoons peanut oil
450g (1 lb) French beans, topped and tailed
1 cm (½ in) piece fresh root ginger, peeled and
    grated
60 ml (2 fl oz/¼ cup) water
1 teaspoon brown sugar
1 teaspoon dark soy sauce
4 spring onions, chopped

In a wok, heat 1 tablespoon peanut oil,
add beans and ginger and stir-fry for 1
minute. Add water and sugar, reduce the
heat and cook for 5-6 minutes until beans
are tender.

Stir in soy sauce then sprinkle with spring
onions and remaining peanut oil.

Serves 4.

BROAD BEANS & BAMBOO SHOOTS

250 g (8 oz) shelled broad beans
1 tablespoon vegetable oil
250 g (8 oz) canned bamboo shoots, sliced
250 ml (8 fl oz/1 cup) Chinese Chicken Stock,
    see page 29
1 teaspoon sea salt
1 teaspoon cornflour (cornstarch) mixture, see
    page 10
1 tablespoon sesame oil

Bring a saucepan of water to the boil, add
broad beans and cook for 8 minutes until
their skins split. Drain and peel off skins.

In a wok, heat vegetable oil, add beans
and bamboo shoots and stir-fry for 2
minutes. Add stock and salt, cover and
simmer for 2-3 minutes. Stir in cornflour
(cornstarch) mixture until thickened.
Serve sprinkled with sesame oil.

Serves 4.

CHOI SUM WITH FERMENTED TOFU

2 tablespoons vegetable oil
250 g (8 oz) Chinese flowering cabbage, washed
    and drained
90 g (3 oz) can fermented tofu
1 teaspoon toasted sesame seeds

In a wok, heat oil and fry cabbage for 1 minute. Using a slotted spoon, remove from wok, drain on absorbent kitchen paper then chop and arrange on a plate. Pour over tofu and sprinkle with sesame seeds.

Serves 4.

Note: Other Chinese cabbages could be substituted if the flowering variety is not available.

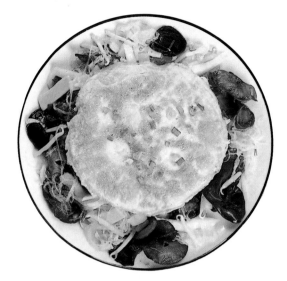

VEGETABLES IN A HAT

4 tablespoons Chinese Chicken Stock
1 tablespoon rice wine or dry sherry
$^1/_2$ teaspoon sea salt
$^1/_4$ teaspoon granulated sugar
60 g (2 oz) dried wood ear mushrooms, soaked in
    hot water for 25 minutes, drained
4 dried black winter mushrooms, soaked in hot
    water for 25 minutes, drained
125 g (4 oz) beansprouts
90 g (3 oz) can bamboo shoots, drained and
    finely chopped
125 g (4 oz) Chinese cabbage, shredded
125 g (4 oz) pea starch noodles, (see Note),
    soaked in hot water for 25 minutes, drained
2 eggs, beaten

In a wok, bring chicken stock, rice wine
or dry sherry, salt and sugar to the boil.
Stir in mushrooms, beansprouts, bamboo
shoots, cabbage and noodles, then simmer for 8 minutes. Drain vegetables and
noodles, place in a warmed serving dish
and keep warm.

In a frying pan, use the eggs to make
Chinese Omelette (see page 24). Place the
Omelette on the vegetables and serve im-
mediately.

Serves 4.

Note: Pea starch noodles are also known
as transparent noodles. Their distinctive characteristic is that they do not become mushy even after prolonged cooking. Soaking before cooking makes the
dish lighter.

-CHINESE MIXED VEGETABLES-

250 g (8 oz) Chinese green vegetables such as choi
   sum, cut into 1 cm (½ in) lengths
90 g (3 oz) can straw mushrooms, drained, liquid
   reserved
90 g (3 oz) can baby sweetcorn, drained, liquid
   reserved
2 large tomatoes, peeled, seeded and sliced
1 tablespoon brown sugar
1 teaspoon cornflour (cornstarch)
1 teaspoon light soy sauce
1 teaspoon sesame oil

Blanch the greens in boiling water for 2 minutes, drain and reserve the liquid. Put the reserved mushroom and sweetcorn liquids in a jug and make up to 250 ml (8 fl oz/1 cup) with the greens water. Sprinkle tomatoes with sugar. In a wok, bring stock to the boil, add tomatoes and simmer for 3 minutes then add the mushrooms and sweetcorn. Simmer for 6 minutes until the corn is heated through. Lift vegetables from stock and arrange on a warmed serving plate; keep warm. Reserve the cooking stock.

To make sauce, in a small bowl, blend together cornflour (cornstarch) and a little of the reserved liquid. In a small saucepan heat the remaining stock and gradually stir in blended cornflour (cornstarch). Bring to the boil, stirring, then simmer until thickened. Stir in soy sauce and sesame oil. Pour over vegetables.

Serves 4.

—BRAISED BAMBOO SHOOTS—

60 g (2 oz/¹/₂ cup) cornflour (cornstarch)
375 g (12 oz) canned bamboo shoots
2 tablespoons vegetable oil
4 slices fresh root ginger, peeled
185 ml (6 fl oz/³/₄ cup) Chinese Vegetable Stock,
    see page 29
1 tablespoon dark soy sauce
1 teaspoon rice wine or dry sherry
1 teaspoon brown sugar
¹/₂ small red pepper (capsicum), thinly sliced
¹/₂ small green pepper (capsicum), thinly sliced
¹/₂ teaspoon sesame oil

Sieve cornflour (cornstarch) onto a plate,
toss in bamboo shoot slices to coat lightly
and evenly. Shake off excess.

In a wok, heat vegetable oil, add ginger,
fry for 1 minute then discard. Add
bamboo shoots, stir-fry for 1 minute then
stir in stock, soy sauce, rice wine or dry
sherry and sugar. Simmer for 5 minutes
until bamboo shoots are just tender. Add
peppers (capsicums) and cook for 3
minutes until softened. Sprinkle with
sesame oil.

Serves 4

— SHANGHAI CASSEROLE —

4 tablespoons peanut oil
185 g (6 oz) broccoli florets
185 g (6 oz) canned bamboo shoots, sliced
185 g (6 oz) carrot, thinly sliced
8 dried black winter mushrooms, soaked in hot
    water for 25 minutes, drained, liquid
    reserved
2 cakes tofu, cut into bite sized pieces
2 teaspoons sea salt
1 teaspoon brown sugar
1 tablespoon dark soy sauce
2 tablespoons rice wine or dry sherry
1 tablespoon cornflour (cornstarch) mixture, see
    page 10

In a saucepan, heat oil, add broccoli, bamboo shoots and carrot, and stir-fry for 3
minutes. Stir in mushrooms with their
soaking liquid and remaining ingredients
except cornflour (cornstarch) mixture and
bring to the boil, stirring.

Reduce heat so liquid simmers, cover and
cook for 15 minutes. If there is too much
liquid, stir in cornflour (cornstarch) mixture and heat, stirring until thickened.

Serves 4.

BROCCOLI WITH MUSHROOMS

750 ml (24 fl oz/3 cups) water
1 cm ($^1/_2$ in) piece fresh root ginger, peeled and
    grated
500 g (1 lb) broccoli florets
12 dried black winter mushrooms, soaked in hot
    water for 25 minutes, drained
1 teaspoon brown sugar
2 tablespoons peanut oil

Sauce:
1 teaspoon oyster sauce
1 tablespoon light soy sauce
1 tablespoon cornflour (cornstarch)
1 teaspoon sesame oil
125 ml (4 fl oz/$^1/_2$ cup) Chinese Vegetable Stock,
    see page 29
ground white pepper

In a saucepan, heat water to the boil;
add ginger and broccoli and boil for 4
minutes. Using a slotted spoon, remove
broccoli and keep warm. Add sugar and
mushrooms to the water, and cook for 6
minutes. Drain well and squeeze out as
much liquid as possible; discard stems.
Place mushrooms in centre of a warmed
serving dish and keep warm.

In a wok, heat peanut oil, add broccoli
and stir-fry for 2-3 minutes. Using a
slotted spoon, remove, drain on absorbent kitchen paper, then arrange around
mushrooms; keep warm.

In a small saucepan, mix together sauce
ingredients, bring to the boil, then simmer, stirring constantly for 3 minutes.
Pour over vegetables.

Serves 4.

— MANDARIN VEGETABLES —

625 ml (20 fl oz/2 ½ cups) Chinese Chicken
  Stock, see page 29
250 g (8 oz) mange tout (snow peas)
125 g (4 oz) carrot, sliced
250 g (8 oz) fresh lotus root, sliced
4 sticks celery, sliced
90 ml (3 fl oz) peanut oil
125 g (4 oz) dried cloud ear mushrooms, soaked
  in hot water for 25 minutes, drained
125 g (4 oz) dried black winter mushrooms,
  soaked in hot water for 25 minutes, drained
500 g (1 lb) Chinese leaves, sliced
2 teaspoons cornflour (cornstarch)
¼ teaspoon brown sugar
½ teaspoon salt
4 Potato Nests, see page 103, to serve

In a large saucepan, heat stock and bring
to the boil, add mange tout, carrot, lotus
root and celery and boil for 3 minutes.
Drain; reserve 125 ml (4 fl oz/½ cup)
stock.

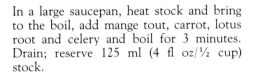

In a wok, heat oil, add mushrooms, then
remaining vegetables and stir-fry for 5
minutes. In a bowl, stir reserved stock
into cornflour (cornstarch) until smooth,
then stir into wok with sugar and salt.
Bring to the boil, stirring, then simmer
until sauce thickens. Serve in Potato
Nests.

Serves 4.

POTATO NESTS

500 g (1 lb) potatoes, finely grated
125 g (4 oz/1 cup) cornflour (cornstarch)
625 ml (20 fl oz/2 ½ cups) vegetable oil

Rinse potatoes in several changes of cold water. Drain well and dry on absorbent kitchen paper. Turn into a bowl and stir in cornflour (cornstarch) to mix thoroughly.

Evenly line a 15 cm (6 in) wire sieve with one quarter of the potato mixture, then cover with another 15 cm (6 in) sieve, so the potato is trapped between the two.

In a wok, heat oil until smoking and lower in the two sieves and deep-fry for 2 minutes until crisp and golden. Lift from oil, allow excess to drain off, then carefully remove the sieves. Keep warm. Repeat with the remaining mixture.

Serves 4.

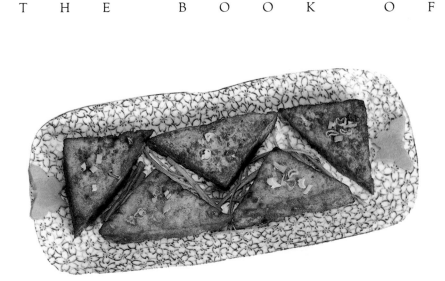

— DEEP-FRIED BEAN CURD —

1 tablespoon sea salt
1 tablespoon Chinese five-spice powder
2 tablespoons granulated sugar
1 teaspoon ground white pepper
1 clove garlic, very finely chopped
4 cakes tofu, halved
625 ml (20 fl oz/2 ½ cups) peanut oil
4 spring onions, very finely chopped

In a bowl, mix together salt, five-spice powder, sugar, pepper and garlic. Add one piece of tofu at a time and turn over to evenly coat. Leave for 1 hour.

In a wok, heat oil until smoking, add tofu and deep-fry curd for 5 minutes until puffy and golden. Drain on absorbent kitchen paper and serve immediately sprinkled with the spring onion.

Serves 4.

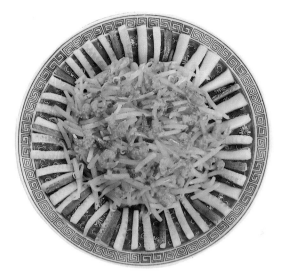

—— SPICED BEANSPROUTS ——

1 kg (2 lbs) beansprouts
185 g (6 oz) cucumber, cut into thin shreds
125 g (4 oz) dried shrimps, soaked in cold water
    for 25 minutes, drained

Sauce:
1 teaspoon light soy sauce
1 teaspoon sea salt
1 cm (½ in) piece fresh root ginger, peeled and
    grated
1 teaspoon ChingKiang vinegar or red wine
vinegar
2 teaspoons sesame oil
½ teaspoon brown sugar

Heat a saucepan of water to the boil. Add beansprouts, return to the boil and cook for 1 minute. Drain, refresh under cold running water, then drain well.

Arrange cucumber around the edge of a plate and put beansprouts in centre. In a bowl, stir together sauce ingredients, then pour over beansprouts. Sprinkle with dried shrimps.

Serves 4.

VEGETARIAN EIGHT TREASURE

2 tablespoons vegetable oil
4 spring onions, sliced
2 cloves garlic, finely chopped
60 g (2 oz) green pepper, (capsicum), seeded and diced
60 g (2 oz) red pepper (capsicum), seeded and diced
2 fresh hot green chillies, seeded and sliced
125 g (4 oz) canned water chestnuts, diced
2 cakes spiced tofu
6 dried black winter mushrooms, soaked in hot water for 25 minutes, drained
125 g (4 oz) cucumber, diced
2 tablespoons black bean paste
1 teaspoon rice wine or dry sherry
1 teaspoon red bean paste
1 teaspoon dark soy sauce
1 teaspoon brown sugar
¼ teaspoon ground white pepper
125 g (4 oz) deep-fried gluten balls, if desired (see note)
2 tablespoons water
1 teaspoon sesame oil to serve

In a wok, heat vegetable oil, add spring onions and garlic, and stir fry for 3-4 minutes until just beginning to colour. Add pepper (capsicum), chillies and water chestnuts; stir-fry for 1 minute. Stir in remaining ingredients except sesame oil and cook for 3 minutes.

Serve sprinkled with sesame oil.

Serves 4.

Note: Deep-fried gluten balls are available in packets in Chinese food shops, and speciality delicatessens.

— VEGETARIAN NEW YEAR —

625 ml (20 fl oz/2 ½ cups) vegetable oil
4 cakes tofu, cut into bite-sized pieces
6 pieces white ji stick (see Note), if desired
60 g (2 oz) dried cloud ear mushrooms, soaked in
    hot water for 20 minutes, drained
60 g (2 oz) dried black winter mushrooms,
    soaked in hot water for 25 minutes, drained
90 g (3 oz) can bamboo shoots, drained and
    sliced
90 g (3 oz) can water chestnuts, drained and
    sliced
60 g (2 oz) golden needles, (see Note), soaked in
    warm water for 10 minutes, drained
60 g (2 oz) shelled ginko nuts, or almonds,
    skinned
1 cake red tofu
1 teaspoon brown sugar
1 tablespoon dark soy sauce

In a wok, heat vegetable oil until smoking,
add tofu and ji sticks, if desired, and fry
for 3-4 minutes until golden and puffy.
Remove and drain on absorbent kitchen
paper. Pour oil from wok leaving just 4
tablespoonsful. Add mushrooms, bamboo shoots, water chestnuts and golden
needles and stir-fry for 5 minutes. Add
nuts, stir-fry for 1 minute then stir in
water. Reduce the heat and simmer for 4
minutes. Add ji sticks.

In a bowl mash together red tofu, sugar
and soy sauce, then stir into wok. Cover
and simmer for 10 minutes; if mixture
begins to dry out, add a little more water.
Stir in deep-fried tofu to heat through.

Serves 4.

Note: Golden noodles are dried lilies
(they may also be called 'tiger lilies'), and
add a subtle flavour.

Note: Ji sticks are strips of bean curd

—— MONKS VEGETABLES ——

3 tablespoons vegetable oil
1 cm (½ in) piece fresh root ginger, peeled and
    grated
2 cloves garlic, finely chopped
125 g (4 oz) beansprouts
12 gingko nuts or almonds, shelled and skinned
125 g (4 oz) broccoli florets
60 g (2 oz) carrots, scraped and sliced
90 g (3 oz) can bamboo shoots, drained and
    sliced
12 canned straw mushrooms
12 button mushrooms
10 dried black winter mushrooms, soaked in hot
    water for 25 minutes, drained
12 deep-fried gluten balls, if desired
2 teaspoons rice wine or dry sherry
1 teaspoon brown sugar
1 teaspoon light soy sauce
125 ml (4 fl oz/½ cup) Chinese Vegetable Stock,
    see page 30
1 teaspoon sesame oil

Sauce:
1 teaspoon cornflour (cornstarch)
1 tablespoon water
½ teaspoon dark soy sauce

In a wok, heat 1 tablespoon vegetable oil, add ginger and garlic, stir-fry for 2 minutes then stir in beansprouts and stir-fry for 1 minute. Remove and keep warm.

Add remaining vegetable oil to wok, heat, then add nuts, broccoli, carrots, bamboo shoots and mushrooms and stir-fry for 2 minutes. Add gluten balls if desired, stir for 1 minute, then stir in remaining ingredients except sesame oil. Reduce the heat and cook gently for 5 minutes.

For the sauce, in a bowl, mix together ingredients, stir into wok and bring to the boil, stirring.   Simmer until thickened. Serve sprinkled with sesame oil.

Serves 4.

Note: Deep-fried gluten balls are available in packets from Chinese food shops and speciality delicatessens.

SHRIMP PASTE RICE

315 g (10 oz) long-grain rice
2 tablespoons shrimp paste
2.5 cm (1 in) piece fresh root ginger, peeled and
    grated
1 tablespoon peanut oil
1 teaspoon sesame oil
2 spring onions, very finely chopped

Cook rice in plenty of boiling water for about 15 minutes until tender but just firm to the bite. Drain then rinse with boiling water.

Meanwhile, in a bowl, mix together shrimp paste, ginger, peanut oil and sesame oil. Transfer rice to a warmed serving bowl and stir in paste mixture. Sprinkle with finely chopped spring onions.

Serves 4.

GREEN FRIED RICE

155 g (5 oz) long-grain rice
3 eggs, beaten
4 tablespoons vegetable oil
250 g (8 oz) spring greens, ribs removed and
    finely sliced
1 clove garlic, finely chopped
4 spring onions, finely chopped
125 g (4 oz) ham, shredded

Cook rice in plenty of boiling water for 15 minutes until tender but still firm to the bite. Drain and rinse with boiling water. Use eggs to make a Chinese Omelette (see page 34); cut it into thin strips.

In a wok, heat 1 tablespoon vegetable oil, add greens and fry for 1 minute; remove and keep warm. Add remaining oil to the wok, add garlic and spring onions and stir-fry for 1 minute, then stir in the rice. When mixed thoroughly, stir in ham, greens, Omelette slices and salt.

Serves 4.

──── CRAB FRIED RICE ────

155 g (5 oz) long-grain rice
3 eggs, beaten
90 g (3 oz) can crab meat
2 tablespoons vegetable oil
185 g (6 oz) beansprouts
1 tablespoon light soy sauce
6 spring onions, finely chopped
1 teaspoon sesame oil

Cook rice in plenty of boiling water for 15 minutes until tender but still firm to the bite. Drain and rinse with boiling water.

In a bowl mix together eggs and crab meat with its liquid. Use to make a Chinese Omelette (see page 24) then cut it into strips.

In a wok, heat vegetable oil, add beansprouts and fry for 1 minute. Remove from wok and keep warm. Add rice to wok and stir-fry for 3 minutes. Stir in soy sauce and cook for a further 2 minutes. Stir in beansprouts, Omelette strips and spring onions, and cook for 2-3 minutes. Serve sprinkled with sesame oil.

Serves 4.

—— VEGETABLE FRIED RICE ——

155 g (5 oz) long-grain rice
4 tablespoons vegetable oil
2 cloves garlic, finely chopped
1 cm (½ in) piece fresh root ginger, peeled and
    grated
1 tablespoon Chinese winter pickle
6 tomatoes, seeded and chopped
1 large red pepper (capsicum), seeded and diced
6 dried black winter mushrooms, soaked in hot
    water from 25 minutes, drained, squeezed
    and diced
60 g (2 oz) cooked peas, or frozen peas, thawed
125 g (4 oz) cucumber, diced
2 tablespoons light soy sauce

Cook rice in plenty of boiling water for 15 minutes until tender but still firm to the bite. Drain and rinse with boiling water.

In a wok, heat oil, add garlic and ginger, fry for 30 seconds then add pickle, tomatoes, pepper (capsicum) and mushrooms, peas and cucumber. Stir-fry for 4 minutes then stir in soy sauce. Add rice, mix well and heat through for 2-3 minutes.

Serves 4.

EGG FRIED RICE

155 g (5 oz) long-grain rice
3 eggs, beaten
2 tablespoons vegetable oil
1 clove garlic, finely chopped
3 spring onions, finely chopped
125 g (4 oz) cooked peas, or frozen, thawed
1 tablespoon light soy sauce
1 teaspoon sea salt

Cook rice in plenty of boiling water for 15 minutes until tender but still firm to the bite. Drain and rinse with boiling water.

In a small saucepan, cook eggs over a moderately low heat, stirring until lightly scrambled. Remove and keep warm.

In a wok, heat oil, add garlic, spring onions and peas and stir-fry for 1 minute. Stir in rice to mix thoroughly, then add soy sauce, eggs and salt. Stir to break up egg and mix thoroughly

Serves 4.

—— YANGCHOW FRIED RICE ——

155 g (5 oz) long-grain rice
3 tablespoons peanut oil
2 medium onions, finely sliced
3 slices fresh root ginger, peeled and finely
    chopped
125 g (4 oz) pork tenderloin, minced
1 tablespoon light soy sauce
1 teaspoon brown sugar
½ teaspoon sea salt
2 eggs, beaten
3 dried black winter mushrooms, soaked in hot
    water for 25 minutes, drained and squeezed
2 large tomatoes, peeled, seeded and chopped
60 g (2 oz) cooked peas, or frozen peas, thawed

Cook rice in plenty of boiling water for 15
minutes until tender but still firm to the
bite. Drain and rinse with boiling water.

In a wok, heat oil, add onion and ginger
and stir-fry for 2 minutes. Stir in pork,
continue stirring for 3 minutes until crisp
then add soy sauce and sugar. Stir-fry for
1 minute, then stir in rice. Remove to a
warmed dish and keep warm. Pour eggs
into wok, season with salt and pepper,
then cook stirring for 2-3 minutes until
just beginning to set. Stir in mushrooms,
tomatoes and peas. Cook for 2-3 minutes,
then stir in rice mixture.

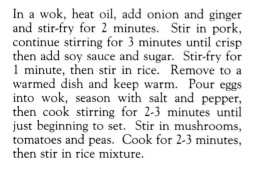

Serves 4.

PEKING APPLES

4 crisp eating apples
125 g (4 oz/1 cup) plain (all-purpose) flour
1 egg
125 ml (4 fl oz/½ cup) water

Syrup:
1 tablespoon vegetable oil
6 tablespoons brown sugar
2 tablespoons golden syrup
2 tablespoons water
iced water to set

In a large bowl, stir the egg and water into the flour to make a thick batter. Peel, core and thickly slice apples. Dip each apple slice in the batter to evenly coat; allow excess to drain off. In a wok, heat oil until smoking. Add apple pieces in batches and deep-fry for 3 minutes until golden brown. Using a slotted spoon, remove to absorbent kitchen paper to drain.

To make syrup, in a small saucepan, gently heat oil, water and sugar, stirring until sugar has dissolved. Simmer for 5 minutes, stirring. Stir in golden syrup and boil for 5-10 minutes until hard and stringy. Reduce heat to very low. Dip each piece of apple into syrup to coat then place in ice cold water for a few seconds. Remove to a serving dish. Repeat with remaining apple. Serve immediately.

Serves 4.

—— CHINESE FRUIT SOUP ——

125 ml (4 fl oz/ ½ cup) rice wine or dry sherry
juice and rind of 2 limes
875 ml (28 fl oz/3 ½ cups) water
250g (8 oz/1 cup) granulated sugar
1 piece lemon grass
4 whole cloves
5 cm (2 in) stick cinnamon
1 vanilla pod, split
pinch ground nutmeg
1 teaspoon coriander seeds, lightly crushed
45g (1 ½ oz) piece fresh root ginger, peeled and
    thinly sliced
30 g (1 oz/ ¼ cup) raisins
500g (1 lb) prepared sweet fruits, eg. mango,
    strawberries, lychees, star fruit, kiwi fruit.

In a saucepan, place rice wine or dry sherry, lime juice and rind, water, sugar, lemon grass, cloves, cinnamon, vanilla, nutmeg, coriander and ginger. Heat gently, stirring until sugar dissolves, then bring to the boil. Reduce heat and simmer for 5 minutes. Leave to cool, then strain into a bowl. Add raisins then chill.

Arrange a selection of prepared fruit in 4 individual serving dishes and spoon over syrup.

Serves 4

— EXOTIC MANGO MOUSSE —

440 g (14 oz) can mandarin segments, drained
440 g (14 oz) can mango pulp
440 ml (14 fl oz/1 3/4 cups) double (thick) cream
45 g (1 1/2 oz) powdered gelatine
90 ml (3 fl oz/1/3 cup) water
4 egg whites
3 tablespoons brown sugar

Reserve a few mandarin segments. In a food processor or blender, process the remaining mandarins until smooth, pour into a measuring jug and add water to make 750 ml (24 fl oz/3 cups).

Turn into a large bowl; stir in mango pulp. In a bowl, whip cream until soft peaks form. Fold into mango mixture until just evenly combined. In a small bowl, sprinkle gelatine over water, leave to soften for 5 minutes then place bowl over a saucepan of boiling water. Stir until gelatine dissolves then remove bowl from heat and allow to cool slightly. Stir in a little of the mango mixture then stir into the large bowl; chill until almost set.

In a clean bowl, whisk egg whites until soft peaks form then whisk in sugar. Carefully fold into mango mixture until just evenly mixed. Serve in individual dishes decorated with the reserved mandarins.

Serves 8.

JASMINE TEA

4 teaspoons jasmine tea
600 ml (20 fl oz/2 ½ cups) boiling water

Put the tea into a warmed tea pot. Pour on the boiling water, stir and leave to infuse for about 4 minutes.

Stir again and pour into cups.

Serves 4.

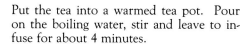

INDEX